D0289313

GIFTS

the joy
of serving
God

GIFTS

the joy of serving God

JOHN ORTBERG

LAURIE PEDERSON

JUDSON POLING

PURSUING SPIRITUAL TRANSFORMATION

WILLOW
Willow Creek Resources

ZONDERVAN™

GRAND RAPIDS, MICHIGAN 49530 USA

ZONDERVAN™

Gifts: The Joy of Serving God
Copyright © 2000 by the Willow Creek Association

Requests for information should be addressed to:

Zondervan, *Grand Rapids, Michigan 49530*

ISBN 10: 0-310-22077-7
ISBN 13: 978-0-310-22077-0

We are grateful for permission given by a number of gifted teachers to use excerpts from their books and messages for the opening readings in the sessions. These authors and speakers are acknowledged throughout this guide.

Interior design by Laura Klynstra Blost

Printed in the United States of America

12 13 14 15 /❖EP/ 21 20 19 18

CONTENTS

Pursuing Spiritual Transformation

The Pursuing Spiritual Transformation series is all about being spiritual. But that may not mean what you think!

Do you consider yourself a spiritual person? What does that mean? Does spiritual growth seem like an impossible amount of work? Do you have a clear picture of the kind of life you'd live if you were to be more spiritual?

Each guide in the Pursuing Spiritual Transformation series is dedicated to one thing—helping you pursue authentic spiritual transformation. Here, the focus is growing through servanthood and the use of your spiritual gifts.

You may find this study different from others you have done in the past. Each week in preparation for your group meeting, you will be completing a Bible study and experimenting with a variety of spiritual exercises. These elements are designed to enhance your private times with God and, in turn, to help you invite him into all aspects of your life, even the everyday routines. After all, spiritual life is just *life*—the one you live moment by moment.

It is very important that you complete this work before going to each meeting because the discussion is based on what you've learned from the study and what you've observed as a result of the spiritual exercise. The Bible study and exercises are not meant to be done an hour before the meeting, quickly filling in the blanks. Instead, we suggest you thoughtfully and prayerfully complete them over the course of several days as part of your regular devotional time with God.

A good modern Bible translation, such as the New International Version, the New American Standard Bible, or the New Revised Standard Version, will give you the most help in your study. You might also consider keeping a Bible dictionary handy to look up unfamiliar words, names, or places. Write your responses in the spaces provided in the study guide or use your personal journal if you need more space. This will help you participate more fully in the discussion, and will also help you personalize what you are learning.

When your group meets, be willing to join in the discussion. The leader of the group will not be lecturing but will encourage people to discuss what they have learned from the study and exercise. Plan to share what God has taught you. Try to be sensitive to the other members of the group. Listen attentively when they speak, and be affirming whenever you can. This will encourage more hesitant members of the group to participate. Be careful not to dominate the discussion. By all means participate, but allow others to have equal time. If you are a group leader or a participant who wants further insights, you will find additional comments in the Leader's Guide at the back of the study.

We believe that your ongoing journey through this material will place you on an exciting path of spiritual adventure. Through your individual study time and group discussions, we trust you will enter into a fresh concept of spiritual life that will delight the heart of God . . . and your heart too!

Ten Core Values for Spiritual Formation

Spiritual transformation . . .

>   . . . is essential, not optional, for Christ-followers.

>   . . . is a process, not an event.

>   . . . is God's work, but requires my participation.

>   . . . involves those practices, experiences, and relationships that help me live intimately with Christ and walk as if he were in my place.

>   . . . is not a compartmentalized pursuit. God is not interested in my spiritual life; he's interested in my *life*—all of it.

>   . . . can happen in every moment. It is not restricted to certain times or practices.

>   . . . is not individualistic, but takes place in community and finds expression in serving others.

>   . . . is not impeded by a person's background, temperament, life situation, or season of life. It is available right now to all who desire it.

>   . . . and the means of pursuing it, will vary from one individual to another. Fully devoted followers are handcrafted, not mass-produced.

>   . . . is ultimately gauged by an increased capacity to love God and people. Superficial or external checklists cannot measure it.

Gifts: The Joy of Serving God

After forty years of faithful service to the company, Jerry was finally getting his reward—a formal retirement banquet held in his honor. When the night arrived, everyone showed up looking their best. White-gloved attendants served all of the meal's courses, but as the night progressed, people looked around nervously. Where was the guest of honor?

After dessert, the CEO of the company got up to speak, awkwardly confessing that no one had seen Jerry. Suddenly, one of the servers came bursting out of the kitchen. Jerry was back there— up to his elbows in soapy water! He had been part of the festivities all night, but he had been waiting on his guests, unrecognized. Now he was doing the dishes.

It's a ridiculous story, right? What guest of honor would spend his moment of glory doing the dirty work for others? "You can be the guest of honor," we'd say, "or you can be the busboy. But you can't be both."

Unless, of course, you're talking about Jesus. At the last banquet Jesus had with his disciples, he was the guest of honor, supreme leader, king—and the towel-wrapped busboy, servant, and foot-washer. The Son of God was also the Son of Man, who did not come to be served, but to serve.

It is perhaps the supreme paradox in God's kingdom. Greatness and servanthood are not simply compatible; they are synonymous. No one will know greatness in his kingdom without knowing servanthood. No one.

Serving may sound like a grudging task we have to gut out by sheer determination. But here we find yet another paradox. God's call to servanthood is a life-giving calling. His brand of servanthood energizes, invigorates, satisfies. And, when he calls, he equips as well. The moment you entrusted your life to him, you received not only cleansing, but charismata—spiritual gifts—that allow you to make a strategic contribution to the body of Christ so that it can become what God intends — a light in a dark world.

One final paradox. When we use our spiritual gifts in a spirit of servanthood, something happens *to* us as well as through us. Old patterns of pride and self-absorption get disrupted. We explore our strengths and come face-to-face with our weaknesses. Failure leads to fresh encounters with grace. Risks lead to fresh experiences of trust. Competitiveness gives way to fresh reliance on community. Serving is a transforming endeavor.

Someday there will be a banquet for you in heaven. You will be welcomed, celebrated, and acknowledged as an honored guest. And if they find you serving in the kitchen, know that right next to you will be the Lord himself, smiling at you with hearty approval . . . towel in hand, joyfully drying the dishes you just washed.

SESSION
ONE

USE ME!

Use Me!

Reading adapted from a message by Bill Hybels

S ome time ago, I had the opportunity to walk through a hundred-year-old hardware store. A man I know had bought it and was showing it to me proudly. He had no idea of the cosmic humor of my being anywhere near a hardware store!

While he was showing me around the store, he pointed to some axes, some sledgehammers, and some shovels that had been made in the early 1900s. For some reason they had never been sold. There they were, sitting on that display shelf, as clean and shiny as the day they were made.

What a shame, I remember thinking. *The sledgehammer should be all beat up and the axe should be on its fifth or sixth handle. These tools should be in someone's garage, and when the owner closes the garage door and the lights go out, the tools ought to be talking to each other about all the posts that had been driven in the ground, the firewood that had been chopped, and the buildings that had been built because they were available to be used. Here they are, on a display shelf, more than eighty years old and not a single story to tell.*

In Ephesians 2:10, Paul talks about you and me. "For we are God's workmanship, created in Christ Jesus to do good works, which God prepared in advance for us to do." Each one of us was designed by God to be a tool that could change the course of human history if we were to be used in the hands of the Master Craftsman.

We sit on the couch and watch the evening news, shaking our heads at the corruption, the violence, the

Each one of us was designed by God to be a tool that could change the course of human history.

greed, the hatred. Imagine how God feels; he designed the world to work in a completely different way!

You need to know that along with God's wrenching heartbreak over the condition of the world is an equally strong determination to turn things around. But long ago, he made the decision not to transform this world with the wave of a heavenly wand. he decided to transform the world through his church—through rank-and-file people like you and me, everyday shovels, rakes, and sledge-hammers in his hands.

This is why one of the most powerful prayers a person can pray is, "Use me, God. Show me what my part is in the transformation of the world. Take hold of my head, my heart, and my hands and use me for your purposes."

Doing Together What No One Could Do Alone

More than twenty-five years ago, a small church youth group that I led found out what happens when you offer up a "use me" prayer.

Long ago, he made the decision not to transform this world with the wave of a heavenly wand.

These students loved the Lord, had an unusual love for one another, and had an intense concern for their unsaved high school friends. Together, we began asking the question, "What would it take to reach those friends?" We held many brainstorming sessions. Ideas started to fly. Before long, we came up with an exciting ministry program. But there was one sobering reality: It would take a lot of work and resources.

I'll never forget when one of the first students spoke up and said, "Well, I can play a musical instrument if that would help." Another said, "I can sing."

We said, "That's great. We need that. You do that."

Another student spoke up: "I can't sing or play an instrument, but I can set up music stands and microphones."

"Great, we need that too."

During one brainstorming session a girl adjusted her chewing gum and said, "Well, did you ever think about using drama?" The blank expression on my face told her that where I came from, people didn't talk much about drama. She explained, "It's where you put on a little skit that's tied into the message you're going to give. If we had drama, the meeting wouldn't just be talk, talk, talk."

"It's all yours."

Another student stepped up. "I'm kind of a leader of people. If we decide to break the group up into subgroups, I could lead one of those." And another said, "I can't do any of that, but I'm artistic. I could make banners and help decorate the gym."

We had one skinny fifteen-year-old kid who asked if he could do the lighting. I didn't know what he was talking about. We already had lightbulbs in the auditorium. He got a bunch of pipes and stood them up, and then got some car headlights—I think he got them off his mother's Buick—and some other spotlights and wired them all together to create stage lighting. Sometimes during the program they'd start sparking and smoking. But we had lights!

We felt the contagiousness of being part of something God was doing that we could never have done individually, but we could do together.

The point is this: Everyone in that original group made a contribution. And do you know what the result was? We felt like everyone in that group really mattered. Not just in the theological sense; each person was important in the practical sense. There was an interdependence, a sense of ownership, a sense of investment.

And everyone shared in the dividends. The group blossomed. Soon there were five hundred students attending, then seven hundred. Ultimately, there were more than one thousand students that emanated out of that original group of twenty-five.

We tasted the joy of servanthood. We tasted what it felt like to count. We felt the contagiousness of being part of something God was doing that we could never have done individually, but we could do together.

Getting Off the Display Rack

God had tremendous plans for that little group of twenty-five. Little did we know that the program we put together would one day become the model for Willow Creek Community Church. But every person had to step up and take a risk. Every one of us had to regularly pray a "use me" prayer.

When was the last time you prayed a "use me" prayer? Have you ever seriously prayed it? God will answer that prayer. He has all throughout history. He will take you off the display rack and he'll start using your life at home, in the workplace, in the neighborhood, and in his church.

He will use your words to encourage people. He will use your mind to inform and counsel people. He will use your heart to show kindness. He will use your hands to serve. And when he does, you'll experience the thrill of being used by God. Nothing I have ever found in this life competes with that thrill. That is why my dream has always been to get to the end of my life and sense that I was completely expended for the sake of God. No tread left on my tires, no shine left on the axe or shovel.

When was the last time you prayed a "use me" prayer? Have you ever seriously prayed it?

In fairness, I must offer a warning: You will get a little "dinged up" over the years. Serving God is not a bed of roses. You take your hits, the shine comes off, and you have to replace parts here and there. Sometimes it's a hurtful thing. But it beats spending your life never experiencing what you were built to do.

You may get beaten up externally, but you will have life and joy and vitality on the inside. You will be full of stories, full of memories. You will be able to recount activities where God used you and other people together to change a little part of the world in some small way, because you were usable in his hands.

I don't think I'm different from you. I think deep down, you too would rather be a tool in the hands of God with the remaining years of your life than be stuck on a shelf, never fulfilling the purpose for which you were built.

But God tends not to commandeer tools. He tends to let them stay on the display shelf until somebody prays, "Use me, God. Use my life." Then the adventure begins.

SPIRITUAL EXERCISE

There is no greater fulfillment than to pour out our lives in acts of servanthood to the God of the universe. This is not limited to certain church activities or involvements. *Every moment* is an opportunity to be used by him. Make this week an adventure by praying the "use me" prayer. Seek to engage in acts of deliberate servanthood. Here are a few ideas:

- Begin each morning by inviting God to use you through the day. Walk through the main events of your upcoming day with him in prayer.
- Make yourself available to be used at home. Look for ways you could be of service to those with whom you live.
- Throughout the day as you begin a conversation, pray a secret "use me" prayer. Listen for God's promptings to encourage others, speak the truth, etc.
- Ask God to use you in the life of a seeker this week.
- Make your work an exercise in being used by God. Work with diligence—as if you were working directly for him. Serve a coworker.
- When you are interrupted, pause to see if this is an opportunity to be used by God through a moment of unplanned servanthood.
- Each time you pull out your wallet or write a check, pray a "use me" prayer with respect to your financial resources. Look for opportunities to give, even in small ways.
- Be available to serve someone who is different than you. Practice seeing them through Jesus' eyes.

Keep track of how the week goes. What difference did it make to live your week this way? Were you surprised by any moments when you really felt used by God? Could you identify anything that held you back or interfered with your ability to be used by him?

BIBLE STUDY

I n Romans 12:1–2 (NRSV), Paul offers one of the richest calls in all of Scripture for Christ-followers to fully abandon their lives to the service of their unimaginably gracious Master. Spend a few moments reading this passage.

1. "I appeal to you therefore, brothers and sisters, by the mercies of God. . . ." For Paul, the call to servanthood is *always* rooted in the love and goodness of God. Why is it so critical for you to know and trust the goodness of God in order to fearlessly offer up a "use me" prayer?

How in touch with the mercies of God are you these days? Spend a few moments dwelling on the diverse ways that his grace has been shown to you in the past month or so. Be concrete, listing as many examples as you can (everyday provisions, relational mercies, answers to prayer, forgiveness, etc.).

2. Paul urges us to "present" or "offer" our bodies.

What is the significance of Paul's word choice? What comes to mind when you think of presenting or offering yourself? How would the passage be different if Paul had chosen more passive wording like, "*Allow* yourself to be a living sacrifice"?

According to John 10:17–18, how did Jesus present himself? What point does he specifically make in verse 18?

NOTE: For readers in Paul's day, the word *present* would have carried additional meaning. It was a technical term in the Old Testament for the offering of sacrifices. When the object sacrificed was presented, it was given up and given over. It passed from the offerer's hand to a new owner.

3. Paul says to "present your bodies." This includes our arms, hands, and legs—and all that they do. This wording encompasses the totality of who we are—our thoughts, longings, passions, energy, time, abilities—our whole identity.

What is the significance of this, particularly in light of our human tendency to compartmentalize our "spiritual life" from our "real life"?

4. What struck you as you read the words "living sacrifice"?

"Living" is precisely what a sacrifice is *not*. How would you explain Paul's oxymoron? (Consider also Jesus' words in John 12:24–26.)

5. Paul goes on to say that this kind of full devotion and surrender to God is your spiritual worship. (Some translations say "your spiritual service of worship." That is because the word used here for worship could be just as easily translated service.)

What does that mean to you? What is the connection between service and worship? Why does Paul view the two as inseparable? What is likely to happen if you try to do one without the other?

NOTE: Paul's word for spiritual is *logikon,* from which we get the word *logic*. It is sometimes translated as reasonable. Paul wants us to know that offering ourselves to God—although it may feel frightening—is, in fact, the only way to real life. When you come to understand the goodness of God and his kingdom, it is the only reasonable course to take. It just makes sense.

---

6. In verse 2, Paul tells us, "do not be conformed to this world, but be transformed by the renewing of your mind." (See also Eph. 4:22–24.)

Why is it so critical for your *mind* to be renewed if you want to live the kind of yielded life that Paul is talking about in this passage? How do our daily attitudes, thoughts, fears, and beliefs affect our sevanthood?

What practices or experiences most help you renew your mind?

NOTE: For the word *transformed*, Paul uses the word *metamorphousthe*, from which we get our word *metamorphosis*. When we sacrifice ourselves rightly, it doesn't lead to death any more than a cocoon leads to the death of the caterpillar. It is, instead, the beginning of life. It is an entrance into the kind of life that God wills for us.

7. Now that you have studied the passage, read it through one more time and personalize it. Rewrite the passage in the space below, inserting your name and phrases about your life as if Paul were speaking directly to you.

8. Spend a few moments in candid reflection. Consider the past year. How well have you lived the truth of Romans 12:1–2? Where have you seen encouraging signs of growth?

Reflect on what holds you back. What, even now, might be hindering your full yieldedness to God and his ability to fully use you?

Is there a pattern of sin in your life that you are keeping hidden or are trying to compartmentalize? If so, describe it.

In what ways do you tend to disconnect your "spiritual life" from your "real life"? How is this hindering God's desire to use you through *all* the moments and activities of your day?

Is your mind-set holding you back? What fears, preoccupations, beliefs, and attitudes keep you from being a yielded servant? Are there telltale signs that your way of thinking is becoming "conformed to this world"?

Is your pace of life curtailing your availability?

End this time with prayer. Present yourself. Offer yourself up to be used by God in worshipful service. Ask for his help in transforming whatever is holding you back. Thank him for his promise that the sacrifice he seeks will lead to life.

TAKE-AWAY

My summary of the main point of this session, and how it impacts me personally:

NOTE: You will fill in this information after your group discussion. Leave it blank until the conclusion of your meeting.

SESSION
TWO

USE MY GIFTS!

Use My Gifts!

Reading adapted from a message by Bill Hybels

I still get tingles up my spine when I read certain passages of Scripture. One passage that is most likely to have that effect on me is Acts 2:42–47:

> *They devoted themselves to the apostles' teaching and to the fellowship, to the breaking of bread and to prayer. Everyone was filled with awe.... All the believers were together, and had everything in common. Selling their possessions and goods, they gave to anyone as he had need.... And the Lord added to their number daily those who were being saved.*

Imagine a church out-performing every institution in society!

There is something so compelling, so inspiring about that account of life in the early church. What seems to reverberate in my spirit are the words *all*, *everyone*, and *together*. A spiritual vitality simply enveloped that early church and infected everyone in it. There is something contagious and exhilarating about being part of a movement, a flood tide, a winning team. All you have to do is think of the Chicago Bulls of the 1990s and you know what I mean.

If polled, I think most of us would say, "Just one time in my life, I'd like to be a part of something like that— something that's functioning optimally, effectively, where individuals periodically submerge their own personal desires and give way to the desires of the movement."

When I read of the early church I get a vision, a sense of what that's like. Imagine, everyone yielded to the Holy

Spirit. Everyone giving liberally. Imagine everyone meeting needs and bearing fruit. Everyone boldly proclaiming grace. Imagine a church outperforming every institution in society!

You Are a Priest

Unfortunately, only a percentage of today's churches fit that picture. For years, I wondered where the breakdown happened. How come at one time in history believers participated so vitally in the church, but now so many merely *attend*? What happened?

In his book *Liberating the Church*, Howard Snyder addresses that question. The reason church participation is down, according to Snyder, is that the church has largely forgotten the doctrine of "the priesthood of all believers." Just in case you're wondering exactly what he means, consider the words Peter spoke to ordinary, rank-and-file believers:

Under the High Priest, Jesus Christ, the Bible says that every true believer is a priest.

> But you are a chosen people, a royal priesthood, a holy nation, a people belonging to God, that you may declare the praises of him who called you out of darkness into his wonderful light. Once you were not a people, but now you are the people of God; once you had not received mercy, but now you have received mercy.
>
> —1 Peter 2:9–10

In the Old Testament, God appointed a few individuals to function as priests to the people of Israel. These individuals would act as "go-betweens" with respect to the people and God. They offered formal prayers on behalf of the people, performed religious functions on their behalf, made atonement for sins on their behalf. But when Jesus came, an amazing thing happened. Jesus declared that he was establishing a New Covenant—a new order.

In this new order, when anyone receives Christ as Savior, he or she is immediately adopted into his family. The Holy Spirit takes up residence, and he or she becomes a priest. Under the High Priest, Jesus Christ, the Bible says that every true believer is a priest.

This has fascinating implications. As priests, every believer has direct access to God. There is no need for a human intermediary. We worship directly to God. We pray directly to God. We confess our sins and receive cleansing directly from God. We have bold access to God in times of need, wherever we are. This is an amazing spiritual reality.

But there is a second implication. A priest has a function to perform for the people. You have a function—a priestly responsibility—to perform for the rest of us. It's a high calling, and is not to be taken lightly. A priest prays for his people, encourages his people, confronts his people, grieves and rejoices with his people.

Tragically, many churches are still functioning under the Old Testament model where the members view the pastor, and perhaps a few staff members, as the priests. The generalized assumption is that they have a special relationship with God that others don't have. It's the job of paid ministers to perform the priestly functions. Rank-and-file members don't have priestly functions. It's this thinking that has left the modern church weak and crippled with an overworked pastor or staff and a boatload of unmet needs. It's a hard thing to change.

Let me ask you: Do you see yourself as a priest? How seriously do you take that role?

Let me ask you: Do you see yourself as a priest? How seriously do you take that role? When a need arises, how inclined are you to ask, "Is there any way I can be a minister—a priest—to this person?" How I long for the day when everyone in the church willingly and enthusiastically puts on their priestly garments. Imagine what it would feel like to be a community of priests!

A Pattern of Giftedness

In addition to our generalized priestly functions, God gives each of us specific, tailor-made functions. The genius behind the church is the concept, authored by God, of *spiritual giftedness*. Just what are spiritual gifts? They are divine enablements—special God-given abilities—that he entrusts to each of his people in order to involve them in the task of advancing his purposes. Simply put, God has made you a specialist in some area of ministry.

The apostle Paul describes spiritual gifts in 1 Corinthians 12. He says there are varieties of gifts but the same Holy Spirit. A variety of ministries—ways that gifts can be expressed—but the same Lord. And a variety of effects or results, but the same God. Spiritual gifts assure a high quality of ministry even with the multiplicity of needs and tasks. Spiritual gifts remind us that the Body is not a one- or two-person show—it's a team.

Paul's words in verse 7 are very important: "*to each one* the manifestation of the Spirit is given for the common good." *Each one.* You are no exception. Every genuine believer is given at least one spiritual gift for the advancement of God's purposes. When God gifted you, he took into account your uniqueness—your background, temperament, likes, passions. As you live consistently with your unique pattern of giftedness, you will make the specific contribution God designed you to make.

Do you have any idea what it means to impart not just your gift but also your own life?

Of course, we're also called to serve in areas where we may not be especially gifted. Regardless of our gift mix, all of us are called to be involved in evangelism, mercy, giving, and others. But we can make special contributions in the areas where we are gifted. To the extent that you pursue the discovery and use of your gifts, you will be a blessing. To the extent that you don't, you rob the Body.

Share Yourself

I want to offer one more challenge. There is a more significant way to make a difference than simply sharing your gift. It is sharing *yourself* while sharing your gift.

Consider these words of Paul to the believers in Thessalonica: "Having thus a fond affection for you, we were well-pleased to impart to you not only the gospel of God *but also our own lives,* because you have become very dear to us" (1 Thess. 2:8 NASB). Do you have any idea what it means to impart not just your gift but also your *own life?* Let me try to illustrate.

There are people with mercy gifts who visit people and say merciful things. And then there are those who *expend* themselves. They crawl under the burden. They enter into the pain and actually absorb some of the affliction in the process. It's an amazing thing to watch.

There are small group leaders who simply lead their group through the session, respond to questions, say a prayer, and go home. And then there are leaders who *impart themselves*—their failures, successes, heartaches, their own spiritual journeys. They share part of their soul, nurturing the group down the path to growth and to becoming "family."

There are ushers who just point people to seats. And then there are ushers who know how to share a little portion of themselves in that instant of contact, conveying the message: "You matter. We're glad you're here."

Grab a robe— you're a priest!

There are people who do youth work. And then there are those who give their lives to creating centers of love for kids.

What do you do? Do you just share your gift, or do you share your gift *and* share yourself? Do you fill a serving role or do you impart your life?

Imagine

Imagine if each of us decided to take our priestly giftedness and responsibilities seriously. Imagine what would happen if that concern was on the front burner of each believer's mind.

I think it would shape the entire "feel" of a Body. A church can be a sterile place where believers just *attend.* It can be a hotel where people check in and check out. Or it can be a home where you feel like you belong because people are sharing their lives with each other, expending themselves for one another, making a difference *together.* The choice is ours.

So, grab a robe—you're a priest!

SPIRITUAL EXERCISE

C ontinue praying the "use me" prayer, but this week focus particularly on your spiritual gifts.

- Set aside a time to thank God that he has gifted you in a unique way. Don't focus on the gifts you don't have; thank him for the ones you do have. Ask him to show you fresh ways to sharpen your gifts or deepen your use of them. (If you are not yet certain of your gifts, pray this prayer anyway—because it's still true! Just add your heartfelt desire to identify those gifts. It's a prayer God is sure to say yes to!)
- Don't allow yourself to fall into the rut of just "doing a task" at church. Boldly ask God to energize and empower your gifts this week as you use them in the body of Christ. Pray for an effectiveness beyond your human ability.
- Share your life as you share your gifts. Impart yourself!
- Look for unplanned ways that God might use your gifts in the everyday course of life. For example, could . . .

  a mercy gift be deployed in your workplace?
  a helps gift find life in the grocery store?
  wisdom or leadership gifts find expression in your neighborhood?
  the gift of encouragement bless a family member?

At the end of the week, set aside some time to jot down your observations. When did you feel most used? What emotions did you experience along the way? Did you learn anything new about yourself or your giftedness?

BIBLE STUDY

1. What thoughts are triggered when you hear the word *priest?* What connotations—positive or negative—does that word carry for you? How were those ideas shaped? How easy is it for you to see yourself as a priest or minister?

Can you think of a time when a member of the body of Christ served as a priest to you in the way the reading described? What specifically did that person do? What impact did it have on you?

2. In addition to our generalized priestly functions, the Holy Spirit gives each of us gifts—divine enablements—to help us carry out the specific role that God calls each of us to play in building his kingdom. Review the following passages. Identify the gifts specifically mentioned, along with any added instructions given (e.g., the purpose of gifts, attitudes concerning gifts, warnings, etc.).

1 Peter 4:10–11
Gifts mentioned

Instruction

Romans 12:3–8
Gifts mentioned

Instruction

NOTE: One of the richest words in the New Testament is the Greek word that Paul uses here to describe spiritual gifts: *charismata*. It derives from the root word *charis*, which is the Greek word for *grace*. We tend to think of God's grace as simply his forgiveness of sin. But it is not limited to that. God's grace is also evident in his unstinting, creative generosity. *Charis* expresses itself in giving. So it is only natural that the gifts God gives to each of us should come to be known as *charismata*—expressions of God's lavishly generous grace.

Our word *charisma* comes from this term. But where we think of charisma as an attractive, magnetic quality that belongs only to a few, God says that *every* one of his redeemed children has charisma. It is inconceivable to Paul that any Christian should be without some gift of grace.

Ephesians 4:1–13
Gifts mentioned

Instruction

1 Corinthians 12:1–11
Gifts mentioned

Instruction

NOTE: Giftedness is never seen as a merely human quality; it is intimately connected to the Spirit. In 1 Corinthians 12:1, Paul does not use the usual term *charismata*. He uses an alternate word, *pneumatikon,* which comes from the word for Spirit *(pneuma)*. Paul wants us to understand clearly that the gifts we have are not of our own devising or choosing. You cannot choose your giftedness any more than you can choose how tall you want to be. You must simply and humbly open yourself to the truth about who you are (and are *not*) designed by God to be. Further, gifts do not exist for the advancement of our own agenda; they are given by the Spirit to be directed by the Spirit.

3. The above lists are probably not exhaustive. Any ability, consistently energized and used by the Holy Spirit to build up the body of Christ, might well be called a spiritual gift. For example, what additional gift (not mentioned previously) did God energize for the building of the Tabernacle (see Ex. 35:30–35)?

4. Below is a concise summary of spiritual gifts, each with a brief description. Check each one that you are sure you have. If you are not sure, put a question mark beside those that you resonate with, or think you might have. (Remember, no believer has all the gifts and everyone has at least one.)

_____ **Administration:** Ability to organize people, tasks, or events to accomplish ministry effectively and efficiently.

_____ **Apostleship:** Ability to start and oversee new churches or ministries.

_____ **Craftsmanship:** Ability to design or construct items for ministry.

_____ **Creative Communication:** Ability to communicate God's truth through a variety of art forms.

_____ **Discernment:** Ability to distinguish between truth and error, various motives, or the presence of evil.

_____ **Encouragement:** Ability to present truth so as to strengthen and comfort those who are wavering.

_____ **Evangelism:** Ability to effectively communicate the gospel in a compelling way.

_____ **Faith:** Ability to act on God's promises with confidence and unwavering belief.

_____ **Giving:** Ability to contribute resources with great cheerfulness and liberality.

_____ **Healing:** Ability to be God's means for moving people toward wholeness.

_____ **Helps (Serving):** Ability to joyfully accomplish practical tasks that serve others and support ministry.

_____ **Hospitality:** Ability to joyfully create an environment that welcomes others and puts them at ease.

_____ **Intercession:** Ability to consistently and passionately, pray on behalf of others.

_____ **Interpretation:** Ability to make known the message given by one speaking in tongues.

_____ **Knowledge:** Ability to bring crucial truth to the body of Christ through biblical insight and understanding.

_____ **Leadership:** Ability to cast vision, motivate, and direct people to collectively accomplish the purposes of God.

_____ **Mercy:** Ability to cheerfully and practically help those who are suffering.

_____ **Miracles:** Ability to authenticate ministry through supernatural actions that glorify Christ.

_____ **Prophecy:** Ability to relevantly proclaim truth in a way that exposes sin and prompts conviction and repentance.

_____ **Shepherding:** Ability to nurture and guide people toward spiritual maturity.

_____ **Teaching:** Ability to clearly explain God's truth and inspire growth in Christ-followers.

_____ **Tongues:** Ability to speak or pray in an unknown language.

_____ **Wisdom:** Ability to apply spiritual insight to specific issues, often in the midst of conflict or confusion.

5. As you have been serving in the body of Christ, have you ever felt you were in the center of the target of who God made you to be? If so, describe that experience.

What evidence was there that God used you in fruitful ways?

To what extent did others affirm that or give you positive feedback?

NOTE: It is possible to overlook a gift you have, or conversely, to assume a pattern of giftedness that isn't really operative. The best safeguard against either of these problems is feedback from others. Our gifts serve the body of Christ, and they are most easily recognized with the help of that body. Be sure to get a lot of input as you seek to identify your pattern of giftedness.

6. If this topic is somewhat new to you, what steps do you think you could take to begin discovering your pattern of giftedness? Of what benefit do you think a trial-and-error approach might be?

NOTE: It may seem obvious, but you can't observe the fruit of ministry without actually doing ministry. You can't know if you have a gift without attempting to employ it and then evaluating what happened. As you seek to identify what gifts you have, be sure you are trying lots of different activities. Then, after seeing you in action, those serving with you will be able to affirm your pattern of giftedness. Remember, it's easier to steer a moving car than a parked one — it's easier to know what you do best by getting out there and trying several different possibilities than by doing nothing.

If you already know what your gifts are, is there any way in which the Spirit is challenging you concerning their current use or further development?

7. As you try to get a better handle on where God wants to use you, it can be helpful to consider not only your gifts but also your ministry passion — specific areas of heightened interest or concern. For example, a mercy gift can find expression in widely different arenas — children's ministry, grief support ministry, ministry with the elderly — depending on your particular interest. Do you have any specific passion areas?

If you are currently serving in a ministry, how well does it align with your passion? Do you sense that passion growing or declining these days?

8. Consider again the challenge to share your life as you share your gifts. Can you identify a few recent serving experiences where you truly imparted yourself? What difference did it make?

PURSUING SPIRITUAL TRANSFORMATION

TAKE-AWAY

My summary of the main point of this session, and how it impacts me personally:

NOTE: You will fill in this information after your group discussion. Leave it blank until the conclusion of your meeting.

SESSION
THREE

Walking into Weakness

Reading adapted from a message by John Ortberg

I want to tell you one of the most profound statements about the human condition I have ever heard. I heard it a long time ago from someone I admired immensely. You probably know him. He loves to sail. He is in great physical condition. He eats unbelievably healthy food. His name is Popeye, the Sailor Man.

There is a little Popeye in each of us.

Whenever Popeye made a mistake or felt inadequate, he would always say the same thing. Do you remember? "I yam what I yam," he would say. Popeye was not a sophisticated guy. He was not in touch with his shadow self or his inner child. He was just a simple, pipe-smoking, tattoo-wearing sailor man. Don't get your hopes up; don't expect too much. "I yam what I yam and that's all that I yam."

Let's look at three truths. The first truth is that God calls us — not just ministers and missionaries. He calls *each* of us. The second truth is that his call will almost certainly take us beyond our comfort zones. The third truth is that we have a way of resisting God's call. There is a little Popeye in each of us.

We voice our objections: "It's beyond my abilities." We plead our inadequacies: "I yam what I yam." But God's call remains. And so you and I will have to find another response.

Turning Aside

Consider the calling of Moses recorded in Exodus chapters 3 and 4. Once upon a time he had had it all. He had been raised in Pharaoh's court, full of promise and potential. But his fairy-tale life ended abruptly one day when, in a fit of anger, Moses killed a man. A murderer and fugitive, his life is now that of a desert nomad. But God is not done with him. God is going to call him.

It's a normal day. Moses is busy tending his flocks. All of a sudden, he sees a fire in a bush—a bush that is burning, but won't burn up. Moses responds, "I must turn aside and look at this great sight, and see why the bush is not burned up."

Those are four very important words: "I must turn aside." I wonder what would have happened if Moses hadn't turned aside. He didn't have to. God didn't force him. He had a busy day, a full agenda. He could have kept going with the sheep and missed his call. He could have missed the Exodus. He could have missed knowing God. But the world was never the same, because Moses turned aside.

You have to wonder. How many times have there been little shrubs on fire, but a great calling was missed just because somebody didn't turn aside?

How many times have there been little shrubs on fire, but a great calling was missed just because somebody didn't turn aside?

Who Am I?

Once Moses turned aside, God was free to issue his call. "I have observed the misery of my people who are in Egypt. I have heard their cry on account of their taskmasters. I know their suffering. So now go. I will send you to Pharaoh to bring my people, the Israelites, out of Egypt."

Moses is not stupid. Pharaoh is the most powerful man on earth, and God is saying, "Go. Tell Pharaoh you're taking his labor force out of his country. Then just walk out."

Moses was quick to object. "Who am I that I should go?" Do you remember when Dana Carvey used to do his George Bush impression? "Not gonna do it! Wouldn't be wise. Wouldn't be prudent." That's Moses' response.

I imagine Moses saying in his heart, "If you had come to me forty years ago, God, when I was young and had

PURSUING SPIRITUAL TRANSFORMATION

power and status and Pharaoh loved me—I could have done something then! But now I'm just a broken-down shepherd in the desert. Who am I that I should go?"

In other words, "I yam what I yam."

Now, I know I've said those words. And so have you. "I can't do it, God. You know my failures. You know my past. You know my weaknesses. Don't get your hopes up. I yam what I yam."

And God says to Moses what God says to you and me and a million other "Moseses" just like us: "Yes, I know who you are. It doesn't matter. Your sin, your limitations, your shortcomings are no longer the ultimate truth about you. You yam what you yam, but you yam not yet what you yam going to be!"

"From this day on, I will be with you," God says to Moses. "You're mine." This is the promise of God's calling. He may take us out of our comfort zone, but never out of his caring hands.

He may take us out of our comfort zone, but never out of his caring hands.

Still, it's not enough. Moses volleys another objection. "I have never been eloquent . . . I am slow of speech and slow of tongue." God responds, in essence, "Where do you think your mouth came from, Moses? Do you think you got it from Mouths-R-Us? It was my creation. And I will fill it with amazing words. I will give you an ability far beyond your own human ability."

What you see here is a kind of foretaste of the distribution of spiritual gifts. God will give Moses an ability beyond Moses' own human powers. When God calls, he always gifts and empowers.

But we are a stubborn species. Moses objects once again: "O my Lord, please send someone else."

This time we are told, "Then the anger of the LORD kindled against Moses." But even now, God is merciful. "What of your brother Aaron, the Levite? I know he can speak fluently." Moses will not have to carry out this mission by himself. He can do it in community. Aaron can help. Later on, God would also send Moses' sister, Miriam. They would be a team. They could do the job together.

Who Are You?

Moses also tried another line of objection with God, "Who are *you?*"

"If I come to the Israelites and say to them, 'The God of your ancestors has sent me,' and they ask me, 'What is his name?' what shall I tell them?"

When Moses asks for God's name, he is not looking for a label for identification purposes. A name is much deeper than that. A name, in the Old Testament, had to do with someone's character. He's asking here about God's character, about his trustworthiness.

In the final analysis, following the call of God is all about trust.

In today's world, if you want immediate access to an important, busy person, you want the number of their private line. It cuts though all the layers of bureaucracy. Your call goes right through. This is what Moses is asking. Will I have access to you—or are you a distant God? What can I tell my people about you—your heart, your power, your availability? Will I get through to you, or will there be barriers? What is your name?

And God pronounces that great name, "I AM."

"I am the God who saw you as a baby hidden in the reeds. I am the God who saw you in the desert when you fled as a fugitive. I am the God of your ancestors. I am the God of infinite power. I am the God who cares for my people."

"Get your hopes up," God, in essence, says. "I am what I am."

This becomes a defining moment in the history of God's dealings with the human race. God says to Moses and to all of his children, "I want to be known. I want you to grow in the knowledge of me and who I am."

If you are going to step out to serve God, you will need to *know* God. This is not primarily a matter of theology. It is a matter of survival. There will be days when his character is all you'll have to hold on to. It's all you will have to trust. In the final analysis, following the call of God is all about trust. It's all about clinging to the character of God in the face of risk, weakness, and possible failure. Fortunately, there will never be a day when clinging to his character is not enough.

The Bush Is Still Burning

There's an interesting thing about the story of Moses. You find out what happened to Moses. You find out what happened to the children of Israel. You find out what happened to Pharaoh and the soldiers. But you never find out what happened to the bush.

I think it's still burning. I think God is still waiting for people to turn aside. I think he's still waiting for people to hear his call and courageously pursue it.

SPIRITUAL EXERCISE

Like Moses, Paul knew what it was like to feel inadequate for ministry. Once again, God countered those fears with his promise of grace and power. This week, continue praying the "use me" prayer, but this time pray "use me in my weakness." Memorize God's response to Paul:

My grace is sufficient for you, for my power is made perfect in weakness.

—2 Corinthians 12:9

Write these words on your heart. Throughout the week, allow your mind to return to them whenever you feel weak. Allow them to give you the strength you need—to have a difficult conversation, to serve at a task for which you feel inadequate, or to boldly witness when you feel like shrinking back. Step out in faith, trembling but trusting. Let Paul's words remind you of the sufficiency of God's grace and the perfection of his power within you.

BIBLE STUDY

1. In Exodus 3:1–4:17, God gives Moses the greatest challenge of his life: to be used by God to lead the nation of Israel out from their slavery to Pharaoh. The reading summarized Moses' objections and God's responses. Review them using the chart below.

Moses' Concern	God's Answer
3:11	3:12
3:13	3:14–15
4:10	4:11–12
4:13	4:14–16

   With which one(s) of Moses' concerns do you identify the most? Why?

2. When it comes to your own servanthood, what are you doing right now that you know you couldn't do apart from the power of God? Be specific.

Based on your response, how high is the "play it safe" factor in your life right now? Are there any ways that you are avoiding risk regarding servanthood?

What holds you back from hearing and boldly following God's call? (Past failures? Your view of God? Being too preoccupied to turn aside?)

3. What negative behaviors are you prone to when you come face-to-face with your weaknesses or your feelings of inadequacy?

_____ I withdraw from others

_____ I want to quit

_____ I "power up" in my own strength

_____ I project a false confidence

_____ I get angry, frustrated, defensive

_____ I am overwhelmed by anxiety

_____ Other:

4. Second Chronicles 20:1—30 records an amazing story of another servant of God—King Jehoshaphat—who came face-to-face with weakness during a time of national crisis. Read the passage and summarize the nature of the crisis.

NOTE: The situation in 2 Chronicles 20 is made more ironic by the fact that these enemies ganging up on Jehoshaphat and the people of Israel (called Judah here) were distant relatives (descendants of Abraham). They had received much kindness earlier in their history. When Israel left Egypt and conquered the Promised Land, the Ammonites and Moabites were spared the destruction brought upon the other nations dwelling there. God specifically told Israel not to seize any of their land. Attacking Judah now was especially grievous given how well they'd been treated in the past and their blood link to these people.

What do you note concerning Jehoshaphat's level of honesty regarding his fears?

What concrete, constructive steps did he take?

Jehoshaphat's response presents one of the clearest pictures of what it means to be used by God trembling but trusting. What is the phrase that so purely expresses this trust in verse 12?

What was God's response? (vv. 15–17)

5. Centuries after Moses and Jehoshaphat, the apostle Paul attended the school of weakness. There he learned a classic paradox of spiritual life. He describes it in 2 Corinthians 12:9–10. What is the essence of that truth?

How would you explain this seeming contradiction?

6. Take a few moments to identify any specific feelings of weakness, inadequacy, or fear that you are currently experiencing with respect to your serving. Be as concrete as possible.

Consider once again God's response to Moses, Jehoshaphat, and Paul. Write a summary of it as if God was speaking to you.

Now write your own expression of trust to God. What would it mean for you to follow him trembling but trusting?

7. From the standpoint of your own spiritual formation, what has been the value of God allowing you to grapple with weakness?

PURSUING SPIRITUAL TRANSFORMATION

TAKE-AWAY

My summary of the main point of this session, and how it impacts me personally:

> NOTE: You will fill in this information after your group discussion. Leave it blank until the conclusion of your meeting.

SESSION FOUR

COMPARISON: THE KILLJOY OF SERVANTHOOD

Comparison: The Killjoy of Servanthood

Reading adapted from a message by John Ortberg

To be loved means to be chosen. The sense of being chosen is one of the very best gifts love bestows on the beloved. It means someone desires to come closer to me, to be on the same side as I am.

To be loved means to be chosen.

Being chosen involves four factors—three of them are positive.

When I am chosen, I am seen as unique. Each human being cries out to be noticed as special, as not just one more of the same.

When I am chosen, I am recognized as someone who has something to contribute. My uniqueness is positive. I have a gift that will make a difference. I have something that will help the team.

When I am chosen, it means somebody wants me. I am not isolated or unconnected. I belong.

When God chooses us, he imparts all the good implied by the choosing.

In our fallen world, however, the term *chosen* has a fourth implication that is not present in the heart of God. In our world, being chosen almost always means to be chosen at the expense of someone else. In our world, the scramble for chosenness becomes a competitive game. And the consolation prize for the losers is a malignant creature known as envy.

A Study in Envy

Early in Jesus' ministry, we're told that the disciples of John the Baptist came to John and said, "Rabbi, that man who was with you on the other side of the Jordan— the one you testified about—well, he is baptizing, and everyone is going to him" (John 3:26).

John's disciples were very concerned because John's ratings were down. For some time he had been the hottest thing on the circuit, but the latest Neilsen ratings confirmed he was in danger of losing his status. If John the Baptist's status were to go down, guess who else's status would go down with it?

John's followers came to him apparently because they were envious of Jesus' success. It seemed as if John's chosenness was now being lost. It was intolerable to them that after John had launched Jesus in the ministry, Jesus should repay them by out-drawing John. They were so upset they could not speak with out exaggeration: " . . . he is baptizing, and *everyone* is going to him."

Just as Jesus knew temptation, so did John. For John, it could have taken this form: "Do something big to win the people back. Adjust your message; change your marketing strategy." But there was another message in the temptation: "Jesus is our opponent. His ministry is your rival. For him to be bigger means you will be smaller, and this is intolerable."

Envy is pernicious. It can extend to everything—even another person's spirituality, giftedness, or servanthood.

The Anatomy of Envy

Envy is the toxic bile of those who believe themselves to be unchosen. Envy is disliking God's goodness to someone else and dismissing God's goodness to me. Envy is desire plus resentment. It not only seeks self-gratification, but it seeks to diminish the one I envy. Envy is pernicious. It can extend to everything—even another person's spirituality, giftedness, or servanthood.

There is envy in me. It makes no sense when it comes to preaching. In preaching, I'm called to tell people to repent, to take up the cross and die to self. How could I be envious because other preachers can call people to die to themselves better than I can call people to die to themselves?

I do not like the envy in me. I would make it go away if I could. But I cannot stop being envious simply by trying hard. Envy can only be healed when I come to live as one who has been chosen by the God who loves each of his children with infinite uniqueness. In the book *Siblings Without Rivalry*, Adele Faber and Elaine Mazlish note that the love that children crave is not to be loved "equally" with siblings; somehow, equal always feels like less. They write, "To be loved *uniquely*—for one's special self—is to be loved as much as we need to be loved."

John the Baptist understood this truth, and his reflection on it captures perfectly his sense of both who he is and who he is not. "I am not the groom," John says. "I am the friend of the groom."

In ancient Jewish weddings, the friend of the groom was his *shoshbin,* something like our best man. The *shoshbin* was in charge of the details of the wedding arrangements. He would often invite the people. He would accompany the groom to the ceremony. Then, on the final night of the wedding, he would stand guard over the tent where the bride waited for her groom. It would be dark, but when the *shoshbin* recognized the groom's voice, he would stand aside and get out of the way. The groom would go into the tent and know the joy of claiming his bride.

In essence, John said to his followers, "The joy that belongs to the friend of the groom is my joy. I sent out the invitations. I was the one who cried in the wilderness, 'Prepare the way of the Lord.' I served the groom. He is my friend. Now he has come to claim his bride. Don't think this is painful to me. I too have joy. If I were to try to seize *his* joy, I would end up with no joy at all. I will not allow envy to destroy my joy."

Consider a man who chose a different road. In the movie *Amadeus,* Antonio Salieri is the court musician whose soul is destroyed by envy. He longs to create music for the ages, for the glory of God, and (not incidentally)

To be loved uniquely— for one's special self— is to be loved as much as we need to be loved.

for his own fame. The pain of his own mediocrity is intensified by the genius of Mozart and doubled because Mozart is portrayed as an impossibly coarse, flippant boor. Salieri's envy drives him to resentment, hatred, betrayal, and deception.

Salieri, like all first-class enviers, believes that God has been unforgivably unfair to him. He believes God had a moral obligation to make him greater than Mozart. Envy always carries with it a sense of being victimized: "You *owe* me," envy says. "I *deserve* this."

The truth is, Salieri had the possibility of a great joy. He did not possess Mozart's gift—but he was offered another. He could have been the one to recognize Mozart's genius, to proclaim it to the world. He could have been the friend of the groom. But he refused this joy. He wanted only to be the groom, and so he ended his life with no joy at all.

Live a life of comparison or competition and you end up with no joy at all.

A Certain Joy

God holds out a certain joy for each of his children. For example, we can all share in the joy of a singer. As the gifted one sings, she shares her gift and we receive it, all of us grateful to our Creator for lavishing this gift and allowing the singer to share it with us. There is, however, one certain way to lose the joy of the listener, and that is to envy the joy of the singer—to wish that you were up there instead of her, to compare your gift to hers, and feel that sinking sensation that the greater another person's gifts or talents, the more you are diminished. Live a life of comparison or competition and you end up with no joy at all.

God holds out joy for each of us. We are all made to do and see things in a unique way—God has designed you to know the joy of being a teacher or helper or encourager or shepherd—and when you find it and offer it up, you will know joy. Likewise, God has made you to know the joy of receiving and celebrating the gifts of those around you. If you offer your gifts and humbly receive the gifts of others, your joy will be made complete. If you don't, if you go through life wishing for joy that belongs to others, you will end up with no joy at all.

John's final comment was this: "He must become greater; I must become less" (John 3:30). This is no statement of resignation or martyrdom; it is the joy of the friend of the groom who realizes the bride has now entered her destiny. This is John's unique participation in the kingdom of God, where the humble become exalted.

There is a reason why Christmas is celebrated December 25. It is not a historical date, of course, but neither was it chosen at random. It was chosen because it is the time of year when days begin to grow longer and lighter. The coming of Christ means the coming of light to the world. Darkness is being rolled back.

Do you know when, in the church calendar year, John the Baptist's birth is celebrated? June 24. That's when the days begin to get shorter and the light begins to lessen. Every year the calendar proclaims again the words of John, though few are aware of it.

"He must become greater; I must become less." In this there is great joy.

"He must become greater; I must become less."

SPIRITUAL EXERCISE

This week is an opportunity for you to slay the dragon of comparison—or at least injure him! This week, make the focus of your prayer, "God, use *others*."

If you want to experience the flow of love as never before, the next time you are in a competitive situation, pray that the others around you will be more outstanding, more praised, and more used of God than yourself. Really pull for them and rejoice for their successes. If Christians were universally to do this for each other, the earth would soon be filled with the knowledge of God's glory.

—Dallas Willard, *The Spirit of the Disciplines*

- Continually ask God to bless the efforts and lives of those around you—in your family, at work, and at church.
- Notice when others succeed and flourish. Celebrate with them by writing a note, giving a word of affirmation, or even giving them a congratulatory gift.
- Brag about somebody's good works to a third party.
- When you notice envy or comparison rising within you, don't berate yourself. Instead:

    Acknowledge it to God.

    Remind yourself that you are fully loved by God—no one else's achievements or life can diminish that.

    Ask for God's help in shifting your focus to the joy of *your* contribution.

    Talk to a trusted Christian friend about the struggle.

Keep track of how this effort goes. How difficult was it to stay focused on others this way? Did it get easier as you went along, or harder? Was there any one person with whom this exercise was most difficult to live out? Did you experience any breakthroughs?

1. What is the most common sin in the Bible? Surely one of the finalists for that contest—if not the winner—has to be envy. That green-eyed monster shows up over and over. As you look over the chart below, you'll see a small sample of just how often and in what forms it occurs. There are also a few gaps in the chart; look up the references in those places so you can fill in the missing information.

Who?	References	How Envy Fits in the Situation
Cain and Abel	Genesis 4:1–8	Cain was envious of God's acceptance of Abel and his offering.
Jacob and Esau	Genesis 25:27–34; 27:1–36	Jacob was envious of his twin brother Esau's relationship with their father, and he tricked him to get the family inheritance and blessing.
Rachel and Leah	Genesis 30:1	

(continued)

Who?	References	How Envy Fits in the Situation
Joseph and his brothers	Genesis 37:3–4	
Miriam and Aaron against Moses	Numbers 12:1–2	Miriam and Aaron envied Moses' special relationship as God's spokesman.
Saul and David	1 Samuel 18:6–9	
Jesus' disciples	Mark 9:33–34	The disciples discussed who is the greatest.
James and John	Mark 10:35–41	
Jesus' enemies	Mark 15:6–11	

2. How would you summarize what Proverbs 27:4 says about envy?

3. Paul lists several sins in Romans 13:13 that all appear to be very serious. Comment on why you think he included envy (jealousy) in this list.

4. James 3:13−16 explains some of the effects of envy. What are those?

   James is blunt about the spiritual source of envy. In what ways is envy ultimately "of the devil" (demonic)?

5. Why do you think the Scriptures contain such dire warnings about envy? Why is it such a big deal?

6. What is one of Jesus' most earnest desires for his followers according to his prayer in John 17:11 and 23?

How does envy thwart the fulfillment of that prayer?

NOTE: Clearly what stands in the way of the oneness Jesus desires for us is comparison and competition. These are forms of pride that C. S. Lewis calls "The Great Sin" in his book *Mere Christianity*. Because of envy, Lewis writes, we get "no pleasure out of having something, only out of having more of it than the next man. We say that people are proud of being rich, or clever, or good-looking, but they are not. They are proud of being richer, or cleverer, or better-looking than others. . . . It is the comparison that makes you proud: the pleasure of being above the rest." There can be no oneness in the body of Christ as Jesus prayed for when competition and envy go unchecked.

7. Considering your own serving experiences, what is your reaction to the following statements?

"Live a life of comparison or competition, and you end up with no joy at all."

"Comparison kills community."

"He must increase, I must decrease."

8. The reading spoke of the role of the *shoshbin*—the friend of the groom. Sometimes, even in our serving, we must find joy in that "runner-up" spot. Are you in a situation like that now in some area of your life? If so, what does that feel like? If not, remember a time when you were there and describe that experience.

9. Sometimes our comparison with others' gifts takes the form of devaluing ourselves rather than overvaluing ourselves. Read 1 Corinthians 12:12–26 and answer the following:

Describe a time when you devalued the gifts God gave you because of someone else's giftedness.

Do you sometimes wish you could have someone else's ministry or giftedness? Why or why not?

What is the difference between admiring someone and envying them?

10. On a scale of 1–5, how content are you with respect to your giftedness and your place of service? (1= highly discontent, 5= completely content) Explain your response.

What would it take for you to be completely at peace with how God gifted you?

TAKE-AWAY

My summary of the main point of this session, and how it impacts me personally:

NOTE: You will fill in this information after your group discussion. Leave it blank until the conclusion of your meeting.

SESSION
FIVE

THE MINISTRY
OF THE MUNDANE

The Ministry of the Mundane

Reading adapted from a message by John Ortberg

Leon, Joseph, and Clyde all suffered from the Messiah complex. Not just a touch of narcissism or a dash of grandiosity. They were three chronic psychiatric patients at a hospital in Ypsilanti, Michigan, diagnosed with "psychotic delusional disorder, grandiose type." Each one maintained he was the reincarnation of Jesus Christ. That he was the central figure around whom the world revolved. The three little messiahs.

A psychologist named Milton Rokeach wrote a fascinating book called *The Three Christs of Ypsilanti* about his attempts to help Leon, Joseph, and Clyde come to grips with the truth about themselves—to quit trying to be the Messiah and settle for just being Leon, Joseph, and Clyde.

With little to lose, Rokeach decided to try an experiment. He put the three men into the same small group. He wanted to see if rubbing up against others who also claimed to be the Messiah might make a dent in their delusion. This led to some interesting conversations. One of the men would claim, "I'm the Messiah. I am on a mission to save the earth."

"How do you know?" Rokeach would ask.

"God told me."

And then one of other men would counter, "I never told you any such thing."

Rokeach spent two years working with them. But change comes very hard to deluded little would-be

But change comes very hard to deluded little would-be Messiahs.

Messiahs. If you want to be your own God, you have to settle for living in a tiny universe where there is only room for one person. Their worlds could grow infinitely bigger if they would be willing to become, in the words of a friend of mine, "appropriately small." To stop being the Messiah sounded terrifying. But it would have been their salvation, if they could have ever tried.

The Oldest Sin

I have my own share of a Messiah complex. It is not the kind that would get me sent to Ypsilanti. But in its own way, it is just as serious and irrational as the dilemma of Leon, Joseph, and Clyde. You have a share as well. In fact, the sin of pride and grandiosity is the oldest one in the Bible. Recall the words of the serpent to Eve, " . . . when you eat of it your eyes will be opened, and *you will be like God . . .*" (Gen.3:5).

At the deepest level, pride is the choice to exclude both God and other people from their rightful place in our hearts.

Pride has many faces. Stubbornness is the pride that causes us to shun correction. It renders us unable to stop defending ourselves. Judgmentalism is the pride that moves us to criticize rather than to serve. Competitiveness is the pride that makes us want to be not just smart and wealthy, but smarter and wealthier than those around us. Self-centeredness is the pride that keeps us, like our three Messiah friends, living in a tiny universe where there is only room for one person.

It is often pride that keeps us from accepting our limitations and weaknesses. Some time ago, I had a run of too much travel, too many meetings, too many talks, and I was fatigued. I expressed this to a friend, looking for some sympathy. He surprised me by asking *why* I choose to live like this. The only honest answer was that, more than anything else, I was running on grandiosity. I was afraid that if I declined opportunities, they would stop coming, and if opportunities stopped coming, I would be less important, and if I were less important, that would be terrible. I didn't want to admit my limitations. I didn't want to admit my need for rest.

PURSUING SPIRITUAL TRANSFORMATION

At the deepest level, pride is the choice to exclude both God and other people from their rightful place in our hearts. Jesus said that the essence of spiritual life is to love God and to love people. Pride destroys our capacity to love. It leads us to exclude rather than embrace.

That Confusing Thing Called Humility

In place of pride, Jesus invites us to a life of humility: "All who humble themselves will be exalted" (Luke 18:14 NRSV). But we have become badly confused about humility.

Humility is not about convincing ourselves—or others—that we are unattractive or incompetent. It is not about "beating ourselves up" or trying to make ourselves nothing. If God wanted to make us nothing, he could have done it.

Humility involves a revolution of the soul, the realization that the universe does not revolve around us. In fact, it brings a kind of relief. It is an immense gift. Humility is the freedom to stop trying to be what we're not, or pretending to be what we're not, and accepting our "appropriate smallness." In Martin Luther's words, humility is the decision to "let God be God."

Humility involves a revolution of the soul, the realization that the universe does not revolve around us.

But right here we meet a difficulty. How on earth can we pursue humility? It is one of those virtues that cannot be attained by trying hard to achieve it. The more we pursue it, the more elusive it becomes. We need a training exercise—a discipline—to help us do eventually what we cannot do right now, even by trying hard.

Following Jesus in the Practice of Servanthood

In *Celebration of Discipline*, Richard Foster writes,

More than any other single way the grace of humility is worked into our lives through the Discipline of service.... Nothing disciplines the inordinate desires of the flesh like service, and nothing transforms the desires of the flesh like serving in hiddenness. The flesh whines against service but screams against hidden service. It strains and pulls for honor and recognition.

Here, as elsewhere in the spiritual life, our teacher is Jesus. The Lord said that he did not come "to be served but to serve" (Matt. 20:28). Many people think of this as a temporary interruption of Jesus' normal experience, which would be to *receive* service. In fact, serving is God's business. I remember a Christian speaker say once that pride is forbidden to human beings, but is okay in God because, after all, he is God. This is wrong. God is the Infinite Servant. Jesus did not come as a servant in spite of the fact that he is God; he came *precisely because of* the fact that he is God.

Jesus knew that his own followers would wrestle with the Messiah complex, so he decided to put them in a small group together. And sure enough, one day they "argued about who was the greatest"(Mark 9:34). Hang out with a group of people long enough, and the Messiah complex will rear its ugly head.

God is the Infinite Servant.

So Jesus took a little child, and had his Leons and Clydes and Josephs gather around. In effect, Jesus said, "Here's your ministry. Give yourselves to those who can bring you no status or clout. You need to help this child not just for her sake but more for your sake. For if you don't, your whole life will be thrown away on an idiotic contest to see who is the greatest. But if you serve her—often and well and cheerfully and out of the limelight—then the day may come when you do it without thinking, 'What a wonderful thing I've done.' Then you will begin serving naturally, effortlessly, for the joy of it. Then you will begin to understand how life in the kingdom works."

The Ministry of the Mundane

What Jesus described might be called the ministry of the mundane. The opportunity is offered to us countless times a day. A colleague asks for help with a project at work. Someone's car stalls by the side of the road. This ministry can happen at home, in the middle of the night when one of the children cries. It can happen in the middle of a traffic jam when we let someone go ahead of us.

A similar form of service might be called the ministry of availability. In the Russian church certain people called *poustinikki* would devote themselves to a life of prayer, withdrawing to the desert to live in solitude, but not in isolation. By custom, the *poustinikki's* latch was always off the door as a sign of availability to his neighbors' needs.

Sometimes in our days we must be interruptible for tasks that are not on our agenda. Periodically we must live with the "latch off the door." Sometimes we need to be available to talk or pray with troubled people—people who we will not be able to "cure" and who can't contribute to our image or ministry success.

Servanthood does not mean doing only mundane tasks. Nor does it mean that our days should be filled with nothing but interruptions. Knowing when to be available takes discernment and wisdom. But, generally speaking, the higher our grandiosity and pride quotient, the greater our need for this ministry.

Periodically we must live with the "latch off the door."

Looking to the Messiah

It turns out that the life we have always wanted—when our wants are purified and true—is a life of humility. We see this most clearly in Jesus himself.

There was no pride or grandiosity in Jesus at all. That is one reason that people had such a hard time recognizing him as the Messiah. Jesus was no Superman. He did not defy his enemies with hands on his hips and bullets bouncing harmlessly off his chest. The whip of the Roman soldiers drew real blood, the thorns pressed real flesh, the nails caused mind-numbing pain, the cross led to actual death. And through it all, he bore with them, served them, forgave them, and loved them to the end.

God's great, holy joke about the Messiah complex is this: Every human being who has ever lived has suffered from it—except one. And he was the Messiah.

SPIRITUAL EXERCISE

As we practice the ministry of the mundane, one of the great spiritual disciplines is secrecy — where we abstain from causing our good deeds to be known (see Matt. 6). In the practice of secrecy, we're given freedom from the need to be noticed, approved of, or impressive. This week, make it your prayer to be used by God, but with a twist: "Use me in secret."

- Write an anonymous note of encouragement to someone who needs it.
- Pray earnestly for someone each day this week — but don't tell them. See what happens.
- Give a gift to someone, or make a contribution to an organization without letting anyone know.
- Do a task for someone at home, work, in your neighborhood, or church, but don't tell anyone you did it.

Observe what happened to *you* in secret while serving others in secret. To what degree did your spirit yearn for some acknowledgment or recognition? How tempted were you to drop a hint? In what ways was it satisfying and joyful? How did this kind of servanthood foster humility?

> NOTE: Jesus here does not make secrecy an absolute rule — in Matthew 5:16, for example, he indicates there is a time to "let your light shine before others" (NRSV). Jesus wants us to use secrecy as a tool to help overcome our need to manage others' opinions of us. It must not be practiced with rigid or legalistic attitudes, but rather — as with all disciplines — engaged in as a voluntary exercise intended for our growth and freedom in Christ.

1. Consider times when you tend to think more of yourself than is accurate or healthy (and we all occasionally do!). What does that look like for you? Here are a few examples of how that might play out:

Action or Attitude	Possible Hidden Pride
I'm a person of conviction and principle.	I know I'm right. I hate it when people challenge or correct me.
I see very clearly where those around me need improvement.	Others are never good enough for me; it's easier to criticize than to serve.
I'm competitive.	I'm not happy if I'm not better than others.
I choose carefully who I spend time with.	I don't like to be around people who are difficult, draining, or different from me.
I'm often overscheduled and have a hard time saying no.	I like to be seen as a person who can "do it all."
I'm independent by nature.	I can't depend on anyone; I don't need others.

Write down any of these (or other) prideful tendencies you have:

2. Consider this statement from the reading: "Pride destroys our capacity to love. It leads us to exclude rather than embrace."

What kind of people do you tend to exclude or keep at arm's length? If possible, actually bring to mind a face or recent situation when you acted with subtle (or not so subtle) attitudes of superiority or exclusivity.

In what specific way was pride at the root of that behavior?

3. Read Luke 18:9–14. Summarize the point of the story and why Jesus told it.

What was at the core of the tax collector's attitude of "appropriate smallness"?

What impact should this have when it comes to attitudes of superiority?

Which of the two men are you more like these days?

4. When you are with a group of people, how do you tend to define who is the greatest in that group?

Jesus' disciples were painfully like us. How do you think they would have defined greatness in Mark 9:33–37?

According to Jesus, what is greatness?

What is the hardest for you to accept about this definition?

5. Richard Foster makes this honest observation: "Whenever there is trouble over who is the greatest there is trouble over who is the least.... Most of us know we will never be the greatest; just don't let us be the least." Describe how this might be true for you.

PURSUING SPIRITUAL TRANSFORMATION

In what way, if any, does this human tendency impact your own servanthood?

6. In Matthew 25:31–46 Jesus offers some enormously challenging words concerning the ministry of the mundane. Carefully review the passage. In what way does this passage most challenge you concerning the subjects of humility, servanthood, and true righteousness?

When was the last time you served someone who might be considered "the least" by our cultural standards?

How would your servanthood be different if you really believed you were serving Jesus as you served others?

7. Jesus is our best example of the ministry of the mundane. Read John 13:1–17. Why do you think this has stood out as one of the most remarkable acts of Jesus ever recorded?

NOTE: Imagine the conditions of the paths and streets in the first century—dusty and dirty, littered with animal refuse. Then imagine most people walking barefoot, or at best wearing open sandals. Such conditions made for less than pleasant feet! It's not hard to understand why footwashing was considered such a demeaning task that even slaves could not be required to do it for their masters! A disciple, though, would sometimes render this service to his teacher or rabbi.

Peter was embarrassed at having Jesus wash his feet. Why do you think this was so?

How do you do at *receiving* mundane service from others? What makes it easy or hard for you? How does being on the *receiving* end help cultivate a spirit of humility in our lives?

8. Describe a current relationship or situation in which you are being called to the ministry of the mundane.

What is one of the hardest aspects of living as Jesus would in that situation?

What specific benefits are coming to your character because of it?

TAKE-AWAY

My summary of the main point of this session, and how it impacts me personally:

NOTE: You will fill in this information after your group discussion. Leave it blank until the conclusion of your meeting.

SESSION
SIX

SERVANTHOOD'S
BELL-SHAPED CURVE

Servanthood's Bell-Shaped Curve

Reading adapted from a message by Bill Hybels

Are you familiar with what is known as a bell-shaped curve? If you aren't, imagine a straight line and then put the Liberty Bell on top of it.

The bell-shaped curve became a phenomenon in the field of statistics and marketing largely because it represents the life cycle of certain kinds of products. Think of eight-track tapes. Introduced in the '60s, they became the rage for music lovers everywhere. By the end of the '70s, however, they were in steep descent. And today . . . well, when was the last time you saw an eight-track section in the music department of any store?

Just remind yourself of CB radios, pet rocks, or leisure suits and you'll have some sense of the reality of bell-shaped curves.

Unfortunately, there are many believers whose charts read like a bell-shaped curve when it comes to Christian service.

Unfortunately, there are many believers whose charts read like a bell-shaped curve when it comes to Christian service. They start off strong, but over time there is a leveling off, then a little decline, and a little more. Many end up where they started—on the bench. The question begs to be asked: *Why?* What causes a servant's decline? What makes people drop out?

Are You Running on the Wrong Fuel?

The Bible explains how motivation for Christian service starts with one's salvation experience. It's out of that love exchange—the realization that God has done for me what I could not do for myself—that an unquenchable divine energy is diffused into the spirit of a new believer. There is an insatiable desire to return love to God. When a person has this kind of fuel supply, he'll keep serving and serving. But if an unhealthy fuel supply seeps in, it's a different story. How do you detect an unhealthy fuel supply?

First, look for telltale signs of a meritorious motivation. It's an amazing thing, but for many believers, it is easier to be saved by grace than it is to live in grace. Over time, a performance mind-set reinfiltrates their lives. They may not even be consciously aware that they are returning to the belief that they can work their way into God's pleasure—that their service can gain them something in the eyes of God that can be obtained no other way.

Do you consistently feel unhealthy pressure or guilt associated with your serving? Do you believe that God will love you more if you serve him more? Are you engaged in nonstop Christian activity believing it is the real mark of "spirituality"? If so, there's a chance you're running on the unhealthy fuel of a meritorious mind-set.

Another unhealthy fuel that some of us run on is the fuel of approval seeking. We want to impress our peers or gain the esteem of leadership. Let's face it: when service gets noticed, it feels good. That's not a bad thing. Affirmation and encouragement are important. But like any addiction, an approval addiction keeps you coming back for more and is never quite satisfied. Are you frequently hurt that you didn't get the pat on the back you wanted? Are you often frustrated that your contribution is not being adequately noticed, particularly by certain people? Is there a drivenness to your service? If so, there's a chance you're running on the faulty fuel of approval seeking.

Have you checked your fuel supply lately? What propels you? What sustains you? If it's a worship response to the grace and goodness of God in your life, that's a renewable energy supply that will last. If you're trying to run on any other kind of fuel, you're going to get disappointed. And you're going to run dry. It's just a matter of time.

Like any addiction, an approval addiction keeps you coming back for more and is never quite satisfied.

Are You Suffering from the Wrong Fit?

Another reason for the serving bell curve is that far too many servants are consistently serving outside their giftedness area. When you discover your spiritual gift and use it properly, you will tend to feel charged up. Certainly, you'll get tired, too, but it will generally be accompanied by a sense of satisfaction. When you're habitually functioning *outside* your area of giftedness, there will be depletion and frustration at almost every juncture.

When my son, Todd, was in grade school, he badly wanted a remote control car. After some months of doing chores and saving money, he went to the store and bought the car. When we got home and took the cover off the box, I broke out into a cold sweat. There must have been a thousand parts—*none of them assembled!* I had an instantaneous migraine. I thought, *This is going to take months; I'm going to hate every minute of it and the car won't run when I'm done!*

I think Todd saw the look on my face and said, "This looks like a job for Uncle Joel!" (Joel is a lifelong friend and extremely skilled mechanically.) So I invited Joel over for dinner one night. After we ate, Todd brought out the box to show off his new toy. Joel took one look and said, "This would be great fun to put together!" He immediately volunteered to take it home and work on it. I hoped that by Christmas he'd have it done.

The next day my office door opened. A car came shooting into the room. Joel had devoted the evening to the project. What was a nightmare for me was a delight for him. He got the joy and I retained my sanity and self-esteem.

Some people find Christ and then dive elbow-deep into rightly motivated service only to find out—somewhat shockingly—that they don't really enjoy the serving. They feel frustrated, underchallenged, or overchallenged. They feel awkward. Their esteem seems to be getting beaten up a lot. So what do many believers do? They follow the old bell-shaped curve. They look for escape routes.

When you're habitually functioning outside your area of giftedness, there will be depletion and frustration at almost every juncture.

God *knows* you. He really does. Inside and out. And he loves you. He wants you to flourish and feel freedom, fulfillment, and fruitfulness. So seek out your giftedness carefully. Study, read, talk to your friends about it. Experiment with different areas of service, trusting and praying that you'll land on one and say, "This is me." There is a certain trial-and-error cycle to spiritual gift usage, so persevere in it.

Are You Comitting to Too Much Service?

A third cause for the bell-shaped curve is too much service. You heard it here. Some believers boast, "I'd rather burn out than rust out." The problem is, either way you're *out*.

We start with a "me first" mind-set and are transformed to a "Father first, others first" mind-set. That is exactly as it should be. But where do *your* needs fit into all of this? A lot of people think you are either self-centered or self*less*. If you are truly selfless all the time, you'll probably end up in an institution. There is some middle ground. It's called *self-care*. It exists for the purpose of preserving your giftedness, sanity, relationships, and body for further service in the future.

Are you doing the work of God in a way that is killing the work of God in you? If so, that's not his plan.

For me, that means some very practical things. I need to pay attention to diet, exercise, and rest, because serving over the long haul takes enormous energy. I need to pursue appropriate recreation and diversions so that my spirit gets refreshed and my batteries recharged.

Following Jesus' example, I need time away from people and alone with God. Time when I feel his love. Time when I listen for his leadings. Time when I recalibrate and say, "It's *not* for men's applause; it's for an audience of One. It's *not* to earn God's favor; by his grace I already have. It's *not* for earthly reward; my Father who sees in secret will reward."

Are you doing the work of God in a way that is killing the work of God *in you*? If so, that's not his plan.

If you don't exercise self-care, it will only be a matter of time until your life shows a descent into exhaustion, broken relationships, burnout, or some other kind of calamity. Maybe you think you're going to be a hero and defy the realities of life. You won't. You'll be a statistic. Another bell-shaped curve.

Breaking the Bell

If you are properly motivated, serving in your gift-edness area, and exercising self-care, then the graph of your servanthood will soar. And that's what God wants. I can't impress that on you enough. He wants you to be a joyful, effective, long-term servant of Christ.

And one day you will hear the words, "Well done, good and faithful servant. Well done!"

SPIRITUAL EXERCISE

The Fourth Commandment: "Observe the Sabbath day by keeping it holy, as the LORD your God has commanded you. Six days you shall labor and do all your work, but the seventh day is a Sabbath to the LORD your God. On it you shall not do any work . . ." (Deut. 5:12–14). In contemporary America, it might just be the most violated of all commandments.

"Long-haul" servants of God know the importance of observing the God-made pattern of work and rest, activity and restoration. Honoring the Sabbath is not about legalistic rule-keeping; it is about allowing the God of the universe—your Shepherd—to regularly restore, recalibrate, and re-create you.

Your challenge this week is to be rigorous about observing a Sabbath rhythm.

- Pick a day that will be your Sabbath this week (it doesn't necessarily need to be Sunday). Begin the night before by telling God that you are setting aside the next day for rest and fellowship with him. Offer in advance a "renew me" prayer, inviting his re-creating work in your life—spiritually, physically, emotionally.
- For that one day, cease your usual work. Let it go.
- Engage in an activity that you enjoy and that breathes life into you (as long as you're not a workaholic going back to your work!). Ask the Lord to be a part of this time with you. Don't strain to make it "spiritual." Enjoy it as you would enjoy spending time with a good friend.
- Get whatever rest you need.
- Set aside some time for worship and prayer. Bring to God anything from your week that may need his perspective, his forgiveness, his redirection. Return to his grace. Relax in it.
- If it feels appropriate, gather to enjoy community with loved ones.
- End the day by thanking God for it. Commit the coming day of work and service to him.

Take notes on how this experience goes. How difficult was it to engage in a day of rest? How foreign was it from your normal experience? Was there something in particular that breathed life into you? What impact did this day have on your usefulness the following week? Did you notice any change in your attitudes, anxiety level, fruitfulness, etc.?

1. Paul encountered a problem with the church at Galatia. Although they had trusted in Christ for their salvation, they were returning to the old legalistic ways of looking at spiritual life from their past. According to Galatians 3:1–3 (and also 2:15–16), what was their problem?

How is that error parallel to the problem of people using what the reading called the wrong fuel of meritorious motivation when serving God?

Do you feel susceptible to this kind of fuel? Does your service tend to flow from grace or from a performance mind-set?

2. In Luke 10:38−42, Jesus visits with Mary and Martha, the sisters of Lazarus. How would you describe the essential difference between how Martha and Mary act in the presence of Jesus?

Although Martha may seem more "Christlike" in her busy service, Luke 10:40 indicates there was no joy in her activity. According to the first few words of the verse, what was the effect of her service on her?

What fuel do you think Martha was using?

Do you feel susceptible to this kind of fuel? Why or why not?

3. In Matthew 23:5–7, Jesus spoke of how the Pharisees served God. According to Jesus in verse 5, what was the fuel they ran on?

Do you feel susceptible to this kind of fuel? Why or why not?

4. Acts 6:1–4 describes a time when some leaders of the church were tempted to get involved outside their gift area. What was the essence of the problem?

How did the church solve the problem?

According to verse 7, what was one effect of allowing the Twelve to serve in the ministry that fit them?

5. What causes someone to step into roles for which they are not gifted? Describe a time when that happened in your life.

What was the outcome?

6. How did Jesus model and teach self-care in Mark 1:35–37 and Mark 6:30–32?

Given how short a time Jesus had on earth, why do you think he occasionally chose to stop ministry and get away from it all?

When you fail to care for yourself, what is the typical cause?

What is the typical result? Be specific.

7. In Deuteronomy 5:12–15, God commands the Israelites to observe the Sabbath. What do you think is the connection between his reminding them of his great power in verse 15, and their need to stop working periodically?

How can the truth that God miraculously and powerfully delivered a whole nation out of slavery help you take a weekly Sabbath rest from your activities?

8. How are you currently doing with the areas mentioned in the reading?

I'm running on the right kind of fuel

| 1 | 2 | 3 | 4 | 5 |

Not True   **Very True**

Comments:

I'm serving in an area that fits me

| 1 | 2 | 3 | 4 | 5 |

Not True   **Very True**

Comments:

I'm practicing self-care

Not True   Very True

Comments:

9. In the space below, draw a bell curve. Where would you place yourself in regards to serving right now?

What do you think the Holy Spirit is prompting you to do so that the bell-shaped curve of service doesn't manifest itself in your life?

TAKE-AWAY

My summary of the main point of this session, and how it impacts me personally:

NOTE: You will fill in this information after your group discussion. Leave it blank until the conclusion of your meeting.

SESSION
SEVEN

ABIDE IN HIM

Abide in Him

Reading adapted from a message by John Ortberg

There is one last truth about servanthood that you need to know. It is a sobering truth that, frankly, I would just as soon hurry over. But it is a truth that we all must know: *It is possible to be busy with service but to bear no fruit at all.*

It would be a tragedy if it happened, but it is possible. And so for all of us overachievers whose drivenness can even extend into the spiritual realm, Jesus offers these words:

I am the true vine, and my Father is the vinegrower. ... Abide in me as I abide in you. Just as the branch cannot bear fruit by itself unless it abides in the vine, neither can you unless you abide in me. I am the vine and you are the branches. Those who abide in me and I in them bear much fruit, because apart from me you can do nothing.

—John 15:1, 4–5 (NRSV)

In the metaphor of the grapevine, when a branch abides, fruit is inevitable. When it does not, fruit is impossible. No matter how fast you run or how hard you try, you can't produce fruit on your own. Jesus is very clear on that.

The task of a branch is almost laughably simple: to stay connected to the vine. Agriculturally, it works like this: Nutrients in the water flow from the soil into the roots of the vine. They travel into the trunk and then are

No matter how fast you run or how hard you try, you can't produce fruit on your own.

carried by little capillary tubes to every branch and into the canes that shoot up new every spring, and ultimately into every leaf. There is unceasing flow of life from the vine to the branch. It never ends.

Arguably, our chief objective in serving can be summed up in one phrase: *Be a good branch.* Stay connected to the Source of life in such a way that you are constantly receiving from him whatever it is that you need to bear fruit—wisdom, rest, encouragement, power, love, joy. It's not complex. But to do so will require frequent wrestling with three questions.

Deciding

Will I decide that abiding in the Vine is my number-one priority as a servant?

Will I decide that abiding in the Vine is my number-one priority as a servant?

You and I make that decision every day. One difference between human branches and grape branches is that you and I have a choice. Jesus highlights this reality with a simple two-letter word: "*If* anyone abides in me. . . ."

Have you chosen to make abiding with God the highest pursuit of your life? One thing is certain, you will not drift into it. We live in a world that is constantly pulling us away from abiding. I believe there is a primary form that this pull takes. The evil one loves to keep us from leading fruitful lives by getting us to lead busy lives instead. He has convinced us that to be busy is to be important. Busyness has become a status symbol.

There's an interesting thing about grapes. It takes about as long to produce a grape today as it did in Jesus' day. Fruitfulness doesn't happen in a hurry. Jesus never said, "Abide with me, but let's do it quickly because I don't have much time." Abiding is a slow word.

A point of clarification is needed here. Some people think that to abide means having unending quiet time while doing nothing but prayer and Bible study twenty-four hours a day. They think they could never abide. Only monks have time to abide. At the very least, abiding will have to wait until some other season of life—after the kids grow up, after retirement, or maybe after death.

Abiding simply means to invite Jesus to walk with you through every moment of your whole life. Certainly, you will need to engage in times of solitude and prayer. But genuine abiding is something we must do all throughout our day.

For example, consider starting every morning with an abiding prayer: "Lord, I invite you to walk with me through this day as I seek to serve you. I am just a branch. Help me to cling to you as the vine." Then—just as the branch has an unseen connection to the roots—so you too can have a secret conversation with God as you walk through your entire day. Pour your heart out in private moments of worship. Ask him for whatever it is you need. Pull away, perhaps for just five minutes in the midst of your day, to reconnect. Listen for his Spirit's promptings.

Pruning. A fruitful branch requires it.

Let each day be a private, intimate, priceless connection between you and God. His life will flow into you. It really will. No one will see it, but it will change the way you act, see, speak, and serve. You will live differently. Fruit will be inevitable.

Submit to His Pruning

If you want to be fruitful, the second question you must wrestle with is: Will you submit to the Gardener's pruning?

Pruning. A fruitful branch requires it. "He cuts off every branch in me that bears no fruit, while every branch that does bear fruit he prunes so that it will be even more fruitful" (John 15:2). How many branches? *Every* one. No fruitful branch gets a free pass from this pruning business.

Vines and branches require heavy pruning. From what would have been forty to sixty canes shooting up, a gardener ruthlessly cuts them back to only five in the wintertime. Of course, to prune is to wound temporarily. But the wound heals. A wise gardener wants the branch to focus every bit of energy on the glorious reason for which it was made — fruit.

You see this pruning in Scripture. A classic example is the rich young ruler. "Sell your possessions and give to the poor. . . . Then come, follow me" (Matt. 19:21). Why did Jesus say that? He didn't say it to hammer the guy. Jesus said it because he saw the fruitful life the ruler could live if he would only release his grip, unclutter his life, and begin abiding with Jesus. So Jesus took out the pruning sheers.

Jesus will do this in your life and in mine. He may convict and prune in the area of sinful behaviors. He may take his shears to attitudes that need to change — pride, envy, approval seeking, discontentment. His pruning may involve your calendar or, like the rich ruler, your checkbook. His pruning may come through the voice of a friend, or through the two-edged sword of his Word. But it will come.

It would be nice if pruning could be done just once and then be over forever. But it is not so. You will have to submit to pruning again and again if you want to be a fruitful branch.

Our spirit is being fed by a constant flow of inner words — thoughts, understandings, and perceptions. Not all of the inner words I feed on are good words.

Feeding

The last question is this: Are you willing to feed on God's Word?

Fruitful branches are nourished by the Vinegrower's words. If you want to abide with Jesus, you will need to immerse yourself in Scripture, especially in the words of Jesus. This is not a matter of studying them simply to know the facts of what he said; you need to feed off them.

Our spirit is being fed by a constant flow of inner words — thoughts, understandings, and perceptions. Not all of the inner words I feed on are good words.

Once during a worship service, there was someone behind me singing so loudly and off-key that it wasn't even funny. I heard notes that I'd never heard before in my whole life. I decided I would turn and look. It wasn't *quite* a dirty look—more like a slightly soiled look. As I turned, I was stopped cold. This loud, off-key voice belonged to a severely disabled person. Thankfully, he had his eyes closed. His head was back, his mouth wide open. His was the least self-conscious worship I have ever seen—a man who had so many reasons to be miserable was instead extolling the goodness of God. I wish the words that had been abiding in me had been the words of Christ in John 15—"Abide in my love. . . . Love one another as I have loved you . . ." (vv. 9, 12 NRSV)—instead of the inner words of my critical, judgmental self.

If we want to bear good fruit, we need to abide in Jesus' words. Maybe what you need to do tomorrow is to take some of Jesus' words and live with them all through the day. Consider the very words, "Abide in my love." Write them down. Put them on the dashboard or on your desk. Let the Lord say those words to you in challenging moments, anxious moments, tender moments, tempting moments. If you live with those words, slowly they will change the way that you live. You won't have to worry about bearing fruit. You simply *will* bear fruit.

Maybe what you need to do tomorrow is to take some of God's words and live with them all through the day.

A Final Thought

There is one last thing, and I almost wish that this was not in the text. These are hard words Jesus says in John 15:6 (NRSV): "Whoever does not abide in me is thrown away like a branch and withers; such branches are gathered, thrown into the fire, and burned."

Jesus is just commenting on how things are. If a grapevine didn't bear fruit, it was useless for anything else. Fruitless branches were gathered and destroyed. Jesus doesn't say this to create inappropriate anxiety in any sincere followers. The point of this teaching is that it is possible to deliberately choose not to abide in Jesus—to reject him as my vine. I can decide that I am going to spend my life connecting to something or someone else.

You don't want to get to the end of your life and say, "I did not abide in Jesus. He was there waiting for me every morning when I awakened, but I had other things to do." You don't want to say, "I was busy. I accomplished a lot. But in the end there was no lasting fruit."

"I am the vine and you are the branches. Abide in me as I abide in you, and you will bear much fruit." In all of life, *this* is the best offer you will ever get.

PURSUING SPIRITUAL TRANSFORMATION

SPIRITUAL EXERCISE

Consider this statement from the reading: "Arguably, our chief objective in serving can be summed up in one phrase: *Be a good branch*."

"Be a good branch." Your exercise this week is to live with that phrase. Post it on your mirror, car visor, refrigerator, desk. Consider snapping a branch off a plant. Keep it in a visible place all week as a reminder of what happens to a disconnected branch. What will it take for you to serve intimately and fruitfully connected to the Vine this week? Here are a few suggestions:

- Consider starting each morning with an abiding prayer. ("Lord, I invite you to walk with me through this day as I seek to serve you. I am just a branch. Help me to cling to you as a vine.")
- Continue to ask God to use you. Listen for his promptings along the way. Look for ways to allow his servanthood to flow through you to others, even in the most mundane aspects of your day.
- Throughout the day, keep a secret conversation going with God. Talk to him often. Engage in private moments of worship. Request his help.
- When you encounter a difficult situation or find yourself becoming frantic, discipline yourself to stop. Remind yourself that what you *most* need in that moment is to be a connected branch. Ask for God to supply the courage, wisdom, and power. Trust him for it.
- As you use your spiritual gifts this week, deliberately pause and ask, "Am I doing this *for* Christ or *with* Christ right now?"

At the end of the week, do a review. What difference did it make to live your life this way? How difficult was it to do? What most helped you stay connected? What most frequently thwarted that effort? What were some of the fruits of this exercise—for you personally and for others? Did staying connected to God cause serving to flow rather than feeling like burdensome work?

BIBLE STUDY

1. Centuries before the coming of Christ, the prophet Isaiah brought a word from God expressing God's desire for his people to be fruitful. Read Isaiah 5:1–7. How does God feel about his vineyard?

   How would you answer the rhetorical question God asks in verse 4?

2. Using a construction metaphor, Paul warned of people who engaged in activities during their lives that would not bear lasting results. Read 1 Corinthians 3:10–15. The assumption is that these people are all Christians, because they have the foundation of Christ in their lives (v. 11). They are all building on that foundation. What is the stated difference?

What would be an example in your own life of service that is "gold, silver, or costly stone"? What about "wood, hay, or straw"?

Do you think "gold, silver, and costly stone" refers primarily to church work? Why or why not?

NOTE: One simple way to understand how to do works that are gold, silver, and costly stone is to answer the question, "Am I abiding in Christ and controlled by the Spirit right now?" For example, if you are simply taking out the trash and you can answer the above question with a yes, then that simple act of service is of the gold, silver, and costly stone variety. On the other hand, if you were preaching to multitudes but at that moment you could not say, "I am abiding in Christ and controlled by the Holy Spirit," then that work—no matter how "spiritual" it appears—is mere wood, hay, and straw.

3. Some of the most sobering words Jesus ever uttered are in Matthew 7:21–23. Would you call the people described in verses 22–23 fruitful based on their activities?

According to verse 23, what were these people missing?

NOTE: To know someone in the sense Jesus uses here is certainly not a matter of merely having correct information about the person (as evidenced by verse 21), but something much richer and more intimate. God wants us to know him in a personal, intimate way, and without that, no other kind of knowing—or doing—matters. Another illustration is found in the French language, where there are two verbs for the word *know*: *savoir,* which is said of facts (but not a person), and *connaitre,* which is personal knowledge of an individual. This latter usage comes closer to what Jesus had in mind here: the personal, two-way connection to someone who abides in him.

Reflect for a moment. Is it possible that you might be busy with some activities for God, yet you are not connected to him as you serve? What would it be like to hear Jesus say to you, "You were busy *for* me, but you didn't live *with* me. I don't really know you"?

4. The reading spoke about the pruning work of God in John 15:2. How have you seen that in your own life at times—perhaps even right now?

Even though intellectually we know pruning is a good thing, why is it still hard when God does it? How can that lead to more effective service?

5. The reading also expressed the importance of feeding on the Word as we abide in him. Read Psalm 1:1–3, then paraphrase its truth.

What is your "delight factor" right now when it comes to God's Word?

Practically speaking, what form could meditating on the Word "day and night" take in your life?

6. One of the surest ways to test the health of our abiding is by looking for the fruit of the Spirit in our serving (Gal. 5:22–23). If we use the *gifts* of the Spirit while abiding in Christ, the *fruit* of the Spirit will be seen. It's a thermometer that doesn't lie. Take a few moments to do an honest assessment of your serving during the past month.

	DECLINING			GROWING	
LOVE	1	2	3	4	5

How tender was your heart toward God and those you served? Toward lost people? Toward "the least"? How often did a critical or judgmental spirit rear its head?

JOY	1	2	3	4	5

Did your service flow freely or did it feel like burdensome work? How high was your irritability factor? How inclined were you to feel like a martyr?

PEACE	1	2	3	4	5

How content were you regarding your giftedness and place of service? How often were you anxious? Did you relate with fellow servants in a way that promoted peace or stirred up conflict?

PATIENCE	1	2	3	4	5

How gracious were you when serving led to frustration? How tolerant were you when someone wasn't performing or responding as you hoped?

KINDNESS	1	2	3	4	5

How often did you encourage and affirm others? Was there a warmth to your servanthood? How readily did you engage in simple acts of kindness?

GENEROSITY	1	2	3	4	5

As you served, did you find yourself doing the minimum required or going above and beyond? How joyfully did you open your wallet to meet a tangible need?

	DECLINING				GROWING
FAITHFULNESS	1	2	3	4	5

Were you a person of your word? Would those around you say you served dependably, consistently, and diligently?

GENTLENESS	1	2	3	4	5

How available were you when someone needed a comforting word or a listening ear? In speaking the truth, were you gracious or harsh? Were you moving too fast to even think of being gentle?

SELF-CONTROL	1	2	3	4	5

Would others say you were a team player or one who imposed opinions in a controlling way? Did you think before speaking? Did your words build up or tear down?

Summarize your conclusions. What one or two areas need the most attention right now?

7. As you end this chapter and this entire study, consider making a pledge that you won't let your life be wasted by activity done without connection to Christ—that you will not allow working *for* him to be a substitute for abiding *in* him. Write out your version of that commitment below and then offer it in prayer to him.

TAKE-AWAY

My summary of the main point of this session, and how it impacts me personally:

NOTE: You will fill in this information after your group discussion. Leave it blank until the conclusion of your meeting.

Leader's Guide

How to Use This Discussion Guide

Doers of the Word

One of the reasons small groups are so effective is because when people are face-to-face, they can discuss and process information instead of merely listening passively. *God's truths are transforming* only to the extent they are received and absorbed. Just as uneaten food cannot nourish, truth "out there"—either in a book or spoken by a teacher—cannot make a difference if it is undigested. Even if it is bitten off and chewed, it must be swallowed and made part of each cell to truly give life.

The spiritual transformation at the heart of this Bible study series can occur only if people get truth and make that truth part of their lives. Reading about sit-ups leaves you flabby; doing sit-ups gives you strong abdominals. That's why in every session, we present group members exercises to do during the week. They also study Scripture on their own in (hopefully) unhurried settings where they can meditate on and ponder the truths that are encountered. Group discussion is the other way we've designed for them to grab hold of these important lessons.

This study is not a correspondence course. It's a personal and group experience designed to help believers find a biblical approach to their spiritual lives that really works. We recognize that people have a variety of learning styles, so we've tried to incorporate a variety of ways to learn. One of the most important ways they will learn is when they meet together to process the information verbally in a group.

Not Question-by-Question

One approach to learning used by some small groups encourages members to systematically discuss *everything* they learn on their own during the group time. Such material is designed so group members do a study and then report what their answers were for each question. While this approach is thorough, it can become boring. The method we've adopted includes individual study, but we do not suggest discussing *everything* in the session when you meet. Instead, questions are given to leaders (hence, this Leader's Guide) to get at the heart of the material without being rote recitations of the answers the members came up with on their own. This may be a bit confusing at first, because some people fill in the blanks, expecting each answer to be discussed, and discussed in the order they wrote them down. Instead, you, as a leader, will be asking questions *based* on their study, but not necessarily numerically corresponding to their study. We think this technique of handling the sessions has the best of both approaches: individual learning is reinforced in the group setting without becoming wearisome.

It is also important that you understand you will not be able to cover all the material provided each week. We give you more than you can use in every session—not to frustrate you, but to give you enough so you can pick and choose. *Base your session plan on the needs of individual members of your group.*

There may be a few times when the material is so relevant to your group members that every question seems to fit. Don't feel bad about taking two weeks on a session. The purpose of this series is transformational life-change, not timely book completion!

Getting Ready for *Your* Group

We suggest that to prepare for a meeting, you first do the study yourself and spend some time doing the spiritual exercise. Then look over the questions we've given you in the Leader's Guide. As you consider your group members and the amount of discussion time you have, ask yourself if the questions listed for that session relate to your group's needs. Would some other questions fit better? We've tried to highlight the main points of each session, but you may feel you need to hit some aspect harder than we did, or not spend as much time on a point. As long as your preparation is based on knowledge of your group, customize the session however you see fit.

As we pointed out, you may have to adapt the material because of time considerations. It is very hard to discuss every topic in a given session in detail—we certainly don't recommend it. You may also only have a limited time because of the nature of your group. Again, the purpose isn't to cover every question exhaustively, but to get the main point across in each session (whatever incidental discussion may otherwise occur). As a guide to your preparation, review the *Primary Focus* statement at the beginning and the *Session Highlights* paragraph at the end of each session's Leader's Guide. They represent our attempt to summarize what we were trying to get across in writing the sessions. If your questions get at those points, you're on the right track.

A Guide, Not a Guru

Now a word about your role as leader. We believe all small groups need a leader. While it is easy to see that a group discussion would get off track without a facilitator, we would like you to ponder another very important reason you hold the position you do.

This Bible study series is about spiritual growth—about Christ being formed in each of us. One of the greatest gifts you can give another person is to pay attention to his or her spiritual life. As a leader, you will serve your group members by observing their lives and trying to hear, in the questions they ask and the answers they give, where they are in their spiritual development. Your discerning observations are an invaluable contribution to their spiritual progress. That attention, prayer, and insight is an extremely rare gift—but it is revolutionary for those blessed enough to have such a person in their lives. You are that person. You give that gift. You can bring that blessing.

People desperately need clarity about spirituality. Someone needs to blow away the fog that surrounds the concept of what it means to live a spiritual life and give believers concrete ideas how to pursue it. Spiritual life is just *life*. It's that simple. Christ-followers must invite God into all aspects of life, even the everyday routines. That is where we spend most of our time anyway, so that is where we must be with God. If not, the Christian life will become pretense, or hypocrisy. We must decompartmentalize life so that we share it all with God in a barrier-free union with him.

We say all this so that you, the leader, can be encouraged in and focused on your role. You are the person observing how people are doing. You are the one who detects the doors people will not let God through, the one who sees the blind spots they don't, the one who gently points out the unending patience of God who will not stop working in us until "his work is completed" (Phil. 1:6). You will hold many secret conversations with God about the people in your group—while you meet, during a phone call, sitting across the table at lunch, when you're alone. In addition to making the meeting happen, this is one of the most important things you can do to be a catalyst for life-change. That is why you're meeting together anyway—to see people become more like Christ. If you lead as a *facilitator* of discussion, not a teacher, and a *listener* rather than the one who should be listened to, you will see great changes in the members of your group.

SESSION ONE

Use Me!

Primary Focus: To see the adventure and fulfillment of being used by the God of the universe to accomplish his purposes.

Remember that these questions do not correspond numerically with the questions in the assignment. We do not recommend simply going over what your group members put for their answers—that will probably result in a tedious discussion at best. Rather, use some or all of these questions (and perhaps some of your own) to stimulate discussion; that way, you'll be processing the content of the session from a fresh perspective each meeting.

1. When it comes to rolling up your sleeves and getting involved in things, are you a joiner, a watcher, or somewhere in between?

2. What shaped your attitude toward service growing up?

3. Do you feel you've had the kind of meaningful involvement in a ministry team similar to what was mentioned in the reading? If so, describe that experience.

4. As you prayed the "use me" prayer this week, did you sense God giving you opportunities? Were there any lessons you learned from this exercise that you could share with the group?

5. *(Regarding question 1 in the Bible study)* What is the connection between our view of God's mercies and how easily we offer ourselves as a living sacrifice?

6. For some people, the idea of being "used" is associated with *misuse*—maybe even *abuse*. So when we talk of being used by God, it may sound threatening, or at least unpleasant. What might help someone struggling with this misconception—or if you experience it, what do you think you need?

7. In your everyday experience, what does it mean to present your body as a living sacrifice? How easy is this for you?

8. *(Regarding question 8 in the Bible study)* Look over your response to the various things that can hold you back from living out

Romans 12:1–2. Share with the group at least one of your hindrances.

9. How would you like to grow in servanthood as a result of this study?

Take-Away: At the conclusion of your discussion each week, take a few minutes to have group members sum up the session and its impact on them by filling in the Take-Away section at the end of each session. Don't tell them what they are supposed to write—let them be true to their own experiences. When they have written their summaries, have everyone share with the others what they wrote. Statements should be similar to the statements in Session Highlights. If you feel the whole group may have missed an important aspect of the session, be sure to bring that up in the closing discussion.

Session Highlights: We were created to be tools useful to the Master Craftsman; our part is to pray a "use me" prayer, which involves offering up all that we are and facing whatever hinders our usability; being used by God is not limited to certain spiritual activities; *every moment* provides an opportunity!

Use My Gifts!

Primary Focus: To recognize our identity as priests and to develop and deploy our spiritual gifts in kingdom service.

1. Growing up, did you see priests or ministers as having a special or more spiritual status with God than other people? How has that view affected your perception of your place in the church?

2. Do you tend to view your giftedness as an exciting endowment or a burdensome requirement? Explain.

3. Did you experience any answers to your "use my gifts" prayer this week? What was the exercise like for you?

4. *(Regarding question 4 in the Bible study)* Which spiritual gifts did you identify on the checklist? How certain are you that they are true of you?

> NOTE: If your group members know each other well, this would be a great time to give each other feedback, affirmation, etc. concerning each other's giftedness. Also, don't be afraid to question people who think they have gifts that they might not. If the gift is there, questioning it won't take it away; and if it isn't there, the person can be helped to see himself or herself more accurately (though there may be some pain in that admission, so be sensitive).

5. Who is a role model for your gift(s)?

6. *(Regarding question 5 in the Bible study)* In your serving, when have you felt you were in the center of the target of who God made you to be? What was that like for you?

7. *(Regarding question 7 in the Bible study)* What areas of passion did you identify?

8. If the subject of spiritual giftedness is somewhat new to you, what might be your next step of discovery? If you are a veteran, what can you do to further develop your gifts or put more of yourself into your area of service?

Be sure that, as the leader, you are helping your group members identify what their next steps are for developing their gifts. (There are many helpful resources available. One that we recommend is a Groupware published by Zondervan called *Network*). These steps will not be the same for everyone. This is one of those times when being a good shepherd means a one-size-fits-all approach won't work! Help each group member know what will make the most sense for his or her personal development.

Session Highlights: We are called to be a community of ministers serving together in the body of Christ; God endows every believer with a pattern of giftedness and passion in order to make a unique contribution; our greatest impact comes when we share our lives as we share our gifts.

SESSION THREE

Walking into Weakness

Primary Focus: To hear and follow God's call — trembling but trusting — even in the face of our inadequacies.

1. Have you ever had a burning-bush experience of God's call? If so, what kind of Moses-like excuses did you use as God led you to serve in areas of weakness? What eventually happened?

2. *(Regarding question 2 in the Bible study)* What are you doing that absolutely requires the power of God? How high is the "play it safe" factor in your life?

3. *(Regarding question 3 in the Bible study)* What is your tendency when you come face-to-face with your human weaknesses or feelings of inadequacy?

4. *(Regarding question 4 in the Bible study)* What was your reaction to Jehoshaphat's prayer in 2 Chronicles 20:12? Share a time when you also prayed a similar prayer in the course of your serving.

5. *(Regarding question 5 in the Bible study)* How would you explain the paradox of Paul's words in 2 Corinthians 12:9–10?

6. *(Regarding question 7 in the Bible study)* What has been the value of God allowing you to wrestle with weakness? How has God used your weakness to allow you to help others?

7. What interesting developments did you observe as you prayed the "use me in weakness" prayer throughout the week?

8. Where are you feeling the need for encouragement from the group regarding an area of service?

NOTE: You will learn much about the personal and spiritual needs of those in your group by how they answer the questions. It might be helpful to take notes on your group members so that you'll be able to pray for and support them accordingly.

Session Highlights: Stepping out to serve God leads to grappling with weakness; instead of shrinking back or leaning solely on human strength, we must convert anxiety to trust; by leaning into the character of God, we progressively come to know his sufficiency and grace—and we grow too.

Comparison: The Killjoy of Servanthood

Primary Focus: To recognize the danger of allowing comparison and envy to sap our joy, even when it comes to giftedness and serving.

1. Describe an early experience of envy for you regarding someone's gifts or abilities.

2. What do you think it would have felt like to be John the Baptist watching Jesus become more popular? Have you ever had a similar experience?

3. For you, is comparison a dragon, a little puppy nipping at your heels, or something in between? Explain.

4. For the spiritual exercise, how hard was it to stay focused on others this week? What impact did this exercise have on you?

5. *(Regarding questions 3–6 in the Bible study)* What do you think is true of God and his desires for us that makes him so "anti-envy"?

6. Have you ever experienced a time when comparison (envy) killed community? Describe.

7. *(Regarding question 9 in the Bible study)* How frequently do you suffer from the comparison problem that *devalues* your contribution or pattern of giftedness? Describe a time when this happened.

8. Are there any gifts that are hard for you to admit you don't have? Explain.

9. Regarding contentedness with how God gifted you, where are you on a scale of 1 to 5 (1 being very dissatisfied and 5 being completely satisfied)? What would help you celebrate and accept your gifts?

Session Highlights: Envy is one of the most pervasive sins; envy can extend even to others' ministries and giftedness; joy comes when we embrace and offer our gifts—accepting who we are and who we are not—and celebrating the gifts of others.

A Word about Leadership: Remember the comments at the beginning of this discussion guide about your role as a leader? About now, it's probably a good idea to remind yourself that one of your key functions is to be a cheerleader—someone who seeks out signs of spiritual progress in others and makes some noise about it.

What have you seen God doing in your group members' lives as a result of this study? Don't assume that they've seen that progress—and definitely don't assume they are beyond needing simple words of encouragement. Find ways to point out to people the growth you've seen. Let them know it's happening, and that it's noticeable to you and others.

There aren't a whole lot of places in this world where people's spiritual progress is going to be recognized and celebrated. After all, wouldn't you like to hear someone cheer *you* on? So would your group members. You have the power to make a profound impact through a sincere, insightful remark.

Be aware, also, that some groups get sidetracked by a difficult member or situation that hasn't been confronted. And some individuals *could* be making significant progress—they just need a nudge. Encouragement is not about just saying nice things; it's about offering *words that urge*. It's about giving courage (en-*courage*-ment) to those who lack it.

So, take a risk. Say what needs to be said to encourage your members toward their goal of becoming fully devoted followers.

SESSION FIVE

The Ministry of the Mundane

Primary Focus: To learn to be like Jesus through practical, everyday servanthood.

1. What do you think kept Jesus, the one true Messiah, from having a prideful "Messiah complex"? What lesson can you apply from his life to your experience?

2. How did the secret service exercise go for you? What did you learn about yourself? When is the desire for recognition a healthy thing, and when is it spiritually harmful?

> NOTE: Some people were raised in a situation where personal recognition was not given and possibly discouraged. Parents and other caretakers may have had good motives not to foster pride, or they may have been less kind. Either way, it is important for people to know that the need for affirmation is not necessarily evil. God will someday say, "Well done, good and faithful servant," and Scripture often reminds us to encourage each other with similar words. But the discipline of secret service helps break the hold of our chronic longing for attention and approval. Be sure to clarify the value of appropriate recognition while stressing the need for us to grow content with serving "an audience of One."

3. *(Regarding questions 1 and 2 in the Bible study)* What areas of possible hidden pride did you relate to? How are you inclined toward attitudes of exclusivity or superiority? How would your spouse or closest friend answer this question concerning you?

4. *(Regarding question 5 in the Bible study)* How did you react to Richard Foster's observation that most of us fear being "the least"? How does that concern show up in your life—even in your serving?

5. *(Regarding questions 6 and 7 in the Bible study)* How did Jesus' words in Matthew 25 and his example in John 13 challenge you?

6. When was the last time you served someone who might be considered "the least" in our culture? What did that feel like? Did it challenge any of your prideful tendencies? Did it *lead* to any pridefulness?

7. How easy is it for you to really *believe* you are serving Jesus as you serve an individual? Can you recall a time when that made the difference in you being able to joyfully offer mundane service?

8. *(Regarding question 8 in the Bible study)* In what relationship or situation are you especially being called to the ministry of the mundane these days? What's the most challenging aspect of that? What impact is it having on your character?

NOTE: In light of the subject matter of this lesson, consider doing a project together as a group. Perhaps someone you know could use a hand with some household task or project. There may be a serving opportunity at church that you could all do together. Or consider signing up for an urban or suburban extension opportunity. Whatever you decide, it would be a great way to "put feet" on the concepts discussed here.

Session Highlights: Pride destroys our ability to love; Jesus, the perfect man, was a perfect servant; mundane service helps cultivate a Christlike spirit of humility; secret service trains us away from our addiction to recognition; biblical servanthood is an ongoing lifestyle, not an occasional event.

SESSION SIX

Servanthood's Bell-Shaped Curve

Primary Focus: To understand and combat the common destroyers of long-term servanthood.

1. If you were to fall victim to the bell-shaped curve of service (or if you already have), what would be the most likely culprit: wrong fuel, wrong fit, or wrong intensity?

2. Which of the wrong kind of fuels are you most susceptible to: meritorious motivation or approval seeking?

3. *(Regarding questions 4 and 5 in the Bible study)* What do you think causes people to step into roles for which they're not gifted? Can you describe a time when that happened in your life?

4. Do you easily structure your schedule so rest and re-creation—a Sabbath—are a part of your normal experience? Why or why not? How did your Sabbath exercise go? How life-giving was it?

5. How is it possible to find rest and, at the same time, be involved in service to others?

6. *(Regarding question 7 in the Bible study)* Why is the reminder of God's power a help when it comes to getting off the treadmill and taking a Sabbath?

7. Where are you on the bell-shaped curve? How is your servanthood energy these days?

8. *(Regarding question 9 in the Bible study)* What are you being prompted to do so that the bell-shaped curve of service doesn't manifest itself in your life?

Session Highlights: God wants Christian service to be a lifelong, life-giving endeavor; we need to stay alert to those things that make a servant's spirit sag: faulty motivation, wrong fit, or lack of self-care; don't let the work of God through you destroy the work of God in you.

NOTE: In the next (final) session there are instructions for a suggested group exercise. That activity will make the last meeting longer—or may require an additional meeting. We urge you to look ahead now at that exercise, since it will probably involve scheduling decisions and will certainly require advanced preparation on your part.

SESSION SEVEN

Abide in Him

Primary Focus: To decide that abiding with Christ will be your number-one priority as a servant.

1. Put into your own words what it means to be a "good branch" and abide in Christ. How does busyness affect your abiding?

2. How did your experiment with abiding go this week? How did it affect your serving? What helped you stay connected?

3. What is the difference between doing some activity *for* God and doing it *with* God?

4. *(Regarding question 2 in the Bible study)* What is an example from your own life of something you believe is "gold, silver, or costly stone"? What about "wood, hay, or straw"?

5. What does Jesus mean when he says his Father "prunes" us? Describe what form that pruning has taken in your life.

6. *(Regarding question 5 in the Bible study)* What form does meditating on the Word "day and night" take for you? Describe your overall health with respect to scriptural intake.

7. *(Regarding question 6 in the Bible study)* What was your general reaction to how you're abiding these days based on the fruit of the Spirit assessment? What are signs for you that you are not connected to the Vine?

8. *(Regarding question 7 in the Bible study)* If you feel comfortable doing so, share with the group the commitment you wrote about staying connected to Jesus.

Final Group Exercise: What follows is a suggested group exercise which can be a meaningful time to confirm each person's giftedness and servant spirit—and end this study in a memorable way.

Before the meeting, purchase some plain white hand towels: one for each person in the group. When you get to the end of your discussion of the session, take out the towels and give one to each group member. Also give each person a permanent marker to draw on the towel. Have enough markers so that everyone can be drawing at once. (You may want to test out the markers beforehand to make sure they'll work on the towels you bought.)

Explain to the group members that Jesus is our ultimate example of servanthood, and that on his final night with his disciples, he took a towel and washed their feet (you may want to reread John 13:1–17). These towels represent our intention to follow his example and serve others with our lives, specifically with our gifts and passion.

Invite the people to write on the towel their top spiritual gift(s) from the list in Session 2. Also, have them note their passion area(s). Encourage them to be creative; those who are more artistic may want to draw pictures or some representation of their pattern of giftedness. If someone is unsure of their spiritual gifts, then have them just indicate their passion areas. If they are still confused, they could simply write, "Use me, Lord" as an expression of their desire.

After everyone has completed writing on their towels, let each person explain the significance of what they wrote (or drew). After each one is done, allow the other group members a chance to affirm the person's statements. Have everyone sign their names somewhere on that towel as a witness to the person's commitment to serve God, his people, and his world with their gifts and passion. Then go to the next person, having the person explain the significance of their towel. As before, have the group members witness the person's commitment with their signatures. Continue until everyone in the group has had an opportunity to share.

When everyone has had their turn, close the meeting in prayer. Emphasize the wonder of our servant-Savior who modeled the kind of life he called us to, and who promises to help us live this way as we abide in him.

Session Highlights: Much service does not necessarily equal much fruit; fruitfulness comes when working *with* Christ, not just *for* Christ; our primary objective is to be a good branch; true abiding produces the *fruit* of the Spirit as we use the *gifts* of the Spirit.

John C. Ortberg Jr. is teaching pastor at Willow Creek Community Church in South Barrington, Illinois. He is the author of *The Life You've Always Wanted* and *Love Beyond Reason*. John and his wife, Nancy, live in the Chicago area with their three children, Laura, Mallory, and Johnny.

Laurie Pederson, a real estate investment manager, is a founding member of Willow Creek Community Church. As an elder since 1978, she has helped shape many of the foundational values and guiding principles of the church. She is cocreator of Willow Creek's discipleship-based church membership process. Laurie lives outside of Chicago with her husband, Scott.

Judson Poling, a staff member at Willow Creek Community Church since 1980, writes small group training materials and many of the dramas performed in Willow Creek's outreach services. He is coauthor of the *Walking with God* and *Tough Questions* Bible study series and general editor of *The Journey: A Study Bible for Spiritual Seekers*. He lives in Algonquin, Illinois, with his wife, Deb, and their two children, Anna and Ryan.

WILLOW
Willow Creek Association

Willow Creek Association
Vision, Training, Resources for Prevailing Churches

This resource was created to serve you and to help you build a local church that prevails. It is just one of many ministry tools that are part of the Willow Creek Resources® line, published by the Willow Creek Association together with Zondervan.

The Willow Creek Association (WCA) was created in 1992 to serve a rapidly growing number of churches from across the denominational spectrum that are committed to helping unchurched people become fully devoted followers of Christ. Membership in the WCA now numbers over 10,000 Member Churches worldwide from more than ninety denominations.

The Willow Creek Association links like-minded Christian leaders with each other and with strategic vision, training, and resources in order to help them build prevailing churches designed to reach their redemptive potential. Here are some of the ways the WCA does that.

- **Prevailing Church Conference**—an annual two-and-a-half day event, held at Willow Creek Community Church in South Barrington, Illinois, to help pioneering church leaders raise up a volunteer core while discovering new and innovative ways to build prevailing churches that reach unchurched people.

- **Leadership Summit**—a once-a-year, two-and-a-half-day conference to envision and equip Christians with leadership gifts and responsibilities. Presented live at Willow Creek as well as via satellite broadcast to over sixty locations across North America, this event is designed to increase the leadership effectiveness of pastors, ministry staff, volunteer church leaders, and Christians in the marketplace.

- **Ministry-Specific Conferences**—throughout each year the WCA hosts a variety of conferences and training events—both at Willow Creek's main campus and off-site, across the U.S. and around the world—targeting church leaders in ministry-specific areas such as: evangelism, the arts, children, students, small groups, preaching and teaching, spiritual formation, spiritual gifts, raising up resources, etc.

- **Willow Creek Resources®**—to provide churches with trusted and field-tested ministry resources in such areas as leadership, evangelism, spiritual formation, spiritual gifts, small groups, stewardship, student ministry, children's ministry, the use of the arts—drama, media, contemporary music—and more. For additional information about Willow Creek Resources® call the Customer Service Center at 800-570-9812. Outside the U.S. call 847-765-0070.

- *WillowNet*—the WCA's Internet resource service, which provides access to hundreds of transcripts of Willow Creek messages, drama scripts, songs, videos, and multimedia tools. The system allows users to sort through these elements and download them for a fee. Visit us online at www.willowcreek.com.

- *WCA News*—a quarterly publication to inform you of the latest trends, resources, and information on WCA events from around the world.

- *Defining Moments*—a monthly audio journal for church leaders featuring Bill Hybels and other Christian leaders discussing probing issues to help you discover biblical principles and transferable strategies to maximize your church's redemptive potential.

- *The Exchange*—our online classified ads service to assist churches in recruiting key staff for ministry positions.

- **Member Benefits**—includes substantial discounts to WCA training events, a 20 percent discount on all Willow Creek Resources®, access to a Members-Only section on WillowNet, monthly communications, and more. Member Churches also receive special discounts and premier services through WCA's growing number of ministry partners—Select Service Providers.

For specific information about WCA membership, upcoming conferences, and other ministry services contact:

Willow Creek Association
P.O. Box 3188, Barrington, IL 60011-3188
Phone: 847-570-9812
Fax: 847-765-5046
www.willowcreek.com

a place where ...
nobody stands alone!

Small groups, when they're working right, provide a place where you can experience continuous growth and community—the deepest level of community, modeled after the church in Acts 2, where believers are devoted to Christ's teachings and to fellowship with each other.

If you'd like to take the next step in building that kind of small group environment for yourself or for your church, we'd like to help.

The Willow Creek Association in South Barrington, Illinois, hosts an annual Small Groups Conference attended by thousands of church and small group leaders from around the world. Each year we also lead small group training events and workshops in seven additional cities across the country. We offer a number of small group resources for both small groups and small group leaders available to you through your local bookstore and Willow Creek Resources.

If you'd like to learn more, contact the Willow Creek Association at 1-800-570-9812. Or visit us on-line: www.willowcreek.com.

continue the transformation ...

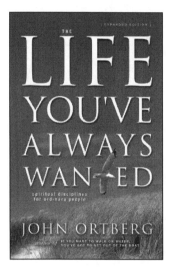

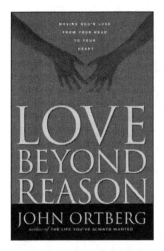

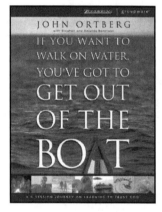

Transform Your Church and Small Groups

Community 101
Gilbert Bilezikian

Written by one of Willow Creek's founders, this resource will help your church become a true community of believers. Bilezikian uses the Bible as his guide to demonstrate the centrality of community in God's plan of salvation and describe how it can be expressed in the daily life of the church.

Softcover – ISBN: 0-310-21741-5

Leading Life-Changing Small Groups
Bill Donahue and the Willow Creek Small Groups Team

Get the comprehensive guidance you need to cultivate life-changing small groups and growing, fruitful believers. Willow Creek's director of adult education and training shares in-depth the practical insights that have made Willow Creek's small group ministry so incredibly effective.

Softcover – ISBN: 0-310-24750-0

Available at your local bookstore!

WILLOW
Willow Creek Resources

ZONDERVAN™
GRAND RAPIDS, MICHIGAN 49530 USA
WWW.ZONDERVAN.COM

www.willowcreek.com